Flexible Fare
Personalize recipes with countless variations

Sandra Rudloff

Bristol Publishing Enterprises
San Leandro, California

Printed in Hong Kong
ISBN 1-55867-228-1

Cover photography: John A. Benson
Cover design: Frank Paredes
Page design: Jennifer Newens
Food styling: Susan Massey
Illustrations: Shanti Nelson
Back cover photography: Carol M. Newman

Acknowledgments

Thanks go to Chris, Jonathan and Stephen Rudloff for their love, patience and their support while I worked on this book; to my mother and late father, Betty and Sylvester Fanucchi, for giving me my love of cooking; to Evonne Fawley for the inspiration and ideas; to everyone at Space Designs, Inc., for their willingness to taste test; and to Jennifer Newens for taking a chance.

Contents

What is Flexible Fare? 1

Breads and Breakfasts 7

Appetizers 27

Salads 47

Soups 61

Side Dishes 79

Entrées 99

Desserts 135

Index 169

What is Flexible Fare?

Are You a Recipe Slave?

Have you seen someone in a supermarket with a copy of a recipe in hand, shopping for the ingredients? Or has someone ever prepared you a meal that you didn't quite like because of one or two ingredients? Are you a "recipe slave?"

One of the first subjects taught at most cooking schools and culinary academies is that a recipe is a template. The ingredients and amounts were chosen by the person who created the recipe to his/her specifications. And of course, not everyone likes the same foods. A great recipe to one may not be to another, simply because of a single ingredient.

Flexible Fare is a cookbook that shows how a recipe can be varied to suit different tastes and available ingredients. Each recipe has at least two variations: an addition, a substitution or an ingredient omitted. By changing one or two items in a recipe, you can create your own signature dishes. But don't be limited by the variations listed. Once you see how easily variations can be made, you can add, change or omit other ingredients to your taste.

There are some ingredients that you should not change, like yeast, baking powder and baking soda, which are critical to the texture of baked goods.

Substitution Tips

The first step to modifying recipes is look for easy substitutions, eliminating one ingredient and using a similar ingredient, using the same quantity and manner. A beginning substitution table is provided to help you understand and give you insight on how to manipulate recipes.

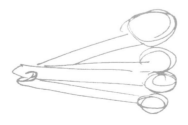

Instead of	Try an equal amount of
apples	pears
artichoke bottoms	asparagus
beef or chicken broth	water or vegetable broth
blackberries	raspberries or strawberries
brandy	sherry
broccoli	cauliflower
canned tomatoes	fresh peeled tomatoes
cantaloupe	honeydew melon
cheddar cheese	Swiss cheese
chicken	turkey
chicken breasts	pork tenderloin
Chinese pea pods	sugar snap peas
chives	green onions
cider vinegar	white vinegar
cinnamon	cardamom, allspice or nutmeg
couscous	tiny pasta (pastina)
cream	half-and-half
crookneck squash	zucchini
dried apricots	dried pears or dried apples
dried basil	dried oregano
fettuccine	spaghetti
ground beef	ground turkey
ketchup	chili sauce
kidney beans	black beans
lemon juice	lime juice
milk chocolate	bittersweet chocolate
mozzarella cheese	provolone cheese
orange juice	grapefruit juice
peaches	pears
pepperoni	salami
pork	chicken breast
raisins	currants or dried cranberries
red potatoes	white potatoes
salmon	swordfish or shark
shrimp	crabmeat
spinach (cooked)	Swiss chard
turnips	parsnips
veal	chicken
walnuts	almonds or pecans
white rice	brown rice or wild rice
yams	sweet potatoes
yellow onions	shallots

3

Omitting and Adding Ingredients

As mentioned, some ingredients should not be omitted or changed, like leavening agents. In reviewing a recipe, it is important to visualize how your omission or addition could change the recipe. Omitting a single ingredient can radically change the taste or texture of a recipe. Adding an ingredient will also change the taste and texture, but could change the quantity of a dish (adding a spice or seasoning would not add much volume, but adding a cup of nuts or an additional vegetable would increase the amount of a dish). When adding or omitting ingredients, it is important to remember that the other ingredients will become more or less prominent.

The variations listed with each recipe show both additions and omissions to the basic recipe. These changes should give an idea of the types of adjustments that can be made. Most of the time, you can combine some of the varied recipes to create another variation of the basic recipe.

It is vital to recognize each ingredient in a recipe as a separate item. The next time you are at a restaurant, try to distinguish the individual tastes of the item you ordered. You may be surprised how easy it will be to recreate restaurant dishes at home once you master this technique.

Breads and Breakfasts

Breads and Breakfasts

Apple Currant Scones 10
Apple Currant Scones with Walnuts
Apple Cranberry Scones
Apricot Scones

Classic Buttermilk Biscuits 11
Sunflower Buttermilk Biscuits
Poppy Seed Buttermilk Biscuits
Buttermilk Biscuits with Chives

Cinnamon-Pecan Rolls 12
Honey Cinnamon Pecan Rolls
Pecan Rolls
Cinnamon Walnut Rolls
Cinnamon Raisin Pecan Rolls
Frosted Cinnamon Pecan Rolls

Cheddar Cheese Muffins 14
White Cheddar Cheese Muffins
Cheddar Cheese and Shallot Muffins

Carrot Raisin Spice Bread 16
Zucchini Raisin Spice Bread
Carrot Nut Spice Bread

Herb Cheese Bread 17
Cheddar Herb Bread
Sun-Dried Tomato and Cheese Bread

Jalapeño Cornbread 18
Green Chile Cornbread
Spicy Chile Cornbread
Bacon and Jalapeño Cornbread

Egg Bread 19
Raisin Egg Bread
Honey Egg Bread

Oatmeal Honey Bread 20
Oatmeal Maple Bread

Rosemary and Garlic Focaccia 21
Pine Nut and Parmesan Focaccia
Sun-Dried Tomato and Garlic
  Focaccia

Rustic Bread 22
Rustic Bread with Olives
Rustic Bread with Walnuts

Potato and Sausage Frittata 23
Potato and Zucchini Frittata
Potato, Sausage and Onion
  Frittata

Summer Frittata 24
Artichoke Frittata
Summer Frittata with Ricotta

Sour Cream Quiche 25
Cheddar and Bacon Quiche
Mexican Quiche
Broccoli Quiche
Spinach Quiche

Apple Currant Scones

These scones have a rustic appearance because they are dropped, rather than rolled out and cut. If you prefer the more traditional triangular scone, lightly flour a work surface and roll the dough out to a 1-inch-thick round. Cut the dough into wedges and bake as directed.

Makes 12-16 Scones

¼ cup apple juice

½ cup dried currants

½ cup finely chopped dried apples

1 cup buttermilk

¼ cup butter, melted and cooled

¼ cup sugar

2 cups all-purpose flour

1 tablespoon baking powder

1 teaspoon baking soda

Preheat oven to 350°.

1 In a small saucepan, bring apple juice to a boil. Stir in currants and apples. Remove from heat, cover pan and let stand for 15 minutes.

2 In a large bowl, combine buttermilk, butter and sugar. Stir in currants, apples and any remaining unabsorbed apple juice. Add flour, baking powder and baking soda. Stir only to mix; do not overmix.

3 Drop ¼ cupfuls of batter onto a baking sheet. Bake until tops are golden, about 14 to 17 minutes. Transfer scones to a wire rack to cool. Store in an airtight container.

Apple Currant Scones with Walnuts
Add ½ cup chopped walnuts in step 2.

Apple Cranberry Scones
Substitute ½ cup dried cranberries for currants in step 1.

Apricot Scones
Omit dried apples and currants. Use 1 cup finely chopped dried apricots in step 1.

Classic Buttermilk Biscuits

A good buttermilk biscuit recipe can be the base for dozens of other variations. Create your own signature biscuits by adding chopped nuts or fresh herbs from your garden.

Makes 10~12 Biscuits

**2 cups
all-purpose flour**

**2 teaspoons
baking powder**

**¼ teaspoon
baking soda**

1 teaspoon salt

**¼ cup vegetable
shortening**

¾ cup buttermilk

Preheat oven to 450°.

1 In a large bowl, mix flour, baking powder, baking soda and salt. With a pastry blender, cut shortening into flour mixture until the mixture resembles coarse crumbs.

2 Add buttermilk and stir with a fork until just mixed, and dough is soft. Transfer dough to a lightly floured work surface and knead 6 or 8 times to finish mixing.

3 Roll out dough to a rectangle about 1/2-inch thick. With a 2-inch biscuit cutter, cut biscuits into rounds.

4 Place biscuits on an ungreased baking sheet and place in oven. Bake until golden, for 12 to 15 minutes.

Sunflower Buttermilk Biscuits
Before adding buttermilk in step 2, add ¼ cup roasted, shelled sunflower seeds.

Poppy Seed Buttermilk Biscuits
Before adding buttermilk in step 2, add 2 tablespoons poppy seeds.

Buttermilk Biscuits with Chives
Before adding buttermilk in step 2, add ¼ cup minced fresh chives.

Cinnamon-Pecan Rolls

Serve warm cinnamon pecan rolls with piping hot coffee for your next Sunday bunch.

Makes 15 Rolls

Dough
½ cup sugar

½ teaspoon salt

3½ teaspoons active dry yeast

4½ - 5 cups all-purpose flour

1 cup milk

½ cup butter, melted

2 eggs

Filling
½ cup brown sugar, packed

1 cup chopped pecans

1½ teaspoons cinnamon

¼ cup butter, melted

Preheat oven to 350°. Spray a 9-x-13-inch baking dish with nonstick spray.

1 To make dough, combine sugar, salt, yeast and 2 cups of the flour in a large bowl; set aside.

2 In a saucepan over medium-low heat, warm milk until it reads 120°-130° on an instant-read thermometer. Remove from heat and add melted butter.

3 With a mixer on low speed, gradually pour milk and butter into the flour mixture. Add eggs. Increase speed to medium and mix for 2 minutes.

4 With a spoon, stir in about 2 to 2½ cups of the remaining flour to make a soft dough (you may not need to use all of the flour.)

5 Transfer dough to a lightly floured work surface and knead with the heals of your hands until smooth, about 10 minutes.

6 Shape dough into a ball and place in a large greased bowl. Cover bowl lightly with a towel and set in a warm place to rise until doubled in size, about 1 hour. Punch down dough. Cover and let rest for 15 minutes while you prepare the filling.

7 To make filling, combine brown sugar, pecans and cinnamon in a small bowl. Set aside.

8 On a lightly floured work surface, roll dough into a 18-x-12-inch rectangle. Brush dough with melted butter and sprinkle evenly with filling.

Glaze (optional)
2 cups
confectioners' sugar

3/4 teaspoon
vanilla extract

3 tablespoons water

9 Starting at the 18-inch side, roll dough jelly roll style. Pinch seams to seal. Slice the dough into 15 slices. Place rolls in prepared pan, cut side down. Cover rolls loosely with a towel and set in a warm place to rise until doubled, about 40 minutes.

10 Place rolls in oven and bake until lightly browned, about 20 to 25 minutes. Remove rolls from oven and cool in pan for 10 minutes. Serve warm.

Honey Cinnamon Pecan Rolls
Use honey instead of sugar in dough. Omit sugar from step 1 and replace with 1/2 cup honey in step 3.

Pecan Rolls
Omit cinnamon.

Cinnamon Walnut Rolls
Use walnuts instead of pecans in step 7.

Cinnamon Raisin Pecan Rolls
Add 1/2 cup raisins to filling in step 7.

Frosted Cinnamon Pecan Rolls
In a small bowl, mix together glaze ingredients until smooth. Frost baked rolls with glaze before serving.

Cheddar Cheese Muffins

M uffins are an easy recipe to have fun with. By adding bacon bits or minced ham you can personalize your own version of these savory muffins

Makes 12 Muffins

2 tablespoons butter

¼ cup minced
fresh chives

2 cups
all-purpose flour

2 teaspoons
baking powder

¾ teaspoon salt

2 tablespoons sugar

2 eggs

1 cup milk

1 cup shredded sharp
yellow cheddar
cheese

Preheat oven to 350°. Prepare a muffin tin by spraying with nonstick spray.

1 Over medium heat, melt butter in a small skillet. Add minced chives and remove from heat; cool to room temperature.

2 In a small bowl, combine flour, baking powder, salt and sugar. Stir to mix; set aside.

3 In a medium bowl, using a wire whisk, combine eggs and milk and whisk until eggs are thoroughly mixed. Add chives, butter mixture and cheddar cheese, stirring to combine. Add flour mixture, stirring only enough to blend thoroughly.

4 Spoon mixture into prepared muffin cups, filling each about 2/3 full. Bake for about 20 to 25 minutes, or until muffin tops just begin to brown. Remove from oven and remove muffins from cups. Cool on a wire rack.

White Cheddar Cheese Muffins
Substitute 1 cup shredded white cheddar cheese for yellow cheddar cheese in step 3.

Cheddar Cheese and Shallot Muffins
Substitute 1 minced shallot for chives in step 1.

Carrot Raisin Spice Bread

This makes a great breakfast bread or lunch box treat. Adding carrots and raisins makes this bread a healthy indulgence.

Makes 1 Loaf

1 ⅓ cups sugar

⅓ cup vegetable shortening

2 eggs

¾ cup shredded zucchini

¾ cup shredded carrots

⅓ cup apple juice

1 teaspoon vanilla extract

½ teaspoon cinnamon

½ teaspoon ground cloves

½ teaspoon ground allspice

1 ⅔ cups all-purpose flour

1 teaspoon baking soda

¼ teaspoon baking powder

¾ teaspoon salt

⅔ cup raisins

Preheat oven to 350°. Prepare a 9-inch loaf pan by greasing and flouring bottom and sides.

1 In a large bowl, mix sugar and shortening until light and fluffy. Add eggs and beat well.

2 Add zucchini, carrots, apple juice, vanilla extract, cinnamon, cloves and allspice. Stir until ingredients are well mixed.

3 In a small bowl, combine flour, baking soda, baking powder and salt. Stir to mix and add to carrot mixture. Stir to mix and add raisins, mixing to incorporate only.

4 Pour batter into prepared pan. Bake for 60 minutes, or until a toothpick inserted into the center comes out clean. Cool in pan for 5 minutes and transfer bread to a cooling rack; cool completely. Store tightly wrapped in the refrigerator.

Zucchini Raisin Spice Bread
Omit carrots. Increase amount of shredded zucchini to 1½ cups in step 2.

Carrot Nut Spice Bread
Omit raisins from step 3 and use ⅔ cup chopped walnuts or pecans.

Herb Cheese Bread

For an easy appetizer, cut this bread into thin slices and serve it with cheese at your next dinner party.

Makes 2 Loaves

2¼ cups all-purpose flour

2 teaspoons baking powder

1 teaspoon salt

½ teaspoon baking soda

2 eggs

3 tablespoons butter, melted and cooled

1¼ cups buttermilk

1 cup shredded Monterey Jack cheese

¼ cup chopped fresh parsley

2 tablespoons chopped fresh chives

1 teaspoon dried basil

1 teaspoon sugar

Preheat oven to 350°. Prepare two 9-inch loaf pans by spraying with nonstick spray.

1 In a medium bowl, combine flour, baking powder, salt and baking soda. Stir to mix.

2 In a large bowl, beat eggs to mix. Add butter and buttermilk and stir to mix. Add cheese, parsley, chives, basil and sugar; stir to mix well.

3 Pour in flour mixture. Mix only enough to moisten. Fill two loaf pans equally with batter and place in oven. Bake for 50 minutes, or until a toothpick inserted in the center comes out clean. Cool in pans for 5 minutes; turn loaves out onto a wire rack to cool. Cool completely before cutting and serving.

Cheddar Herb Bread
Omit Monterey Jack cheese and replace with 1 cup shredded sharp cheddar cheese instead in step 2.

Sun-Dried Tomato and Cheese Bread
Omit parsley and basil in step 2 and add ¼ cup minced sun-dried tomatoes in step 2.

Jalapeño Cornbread

Serve this bread warm with whipped sweet butter. This bread has a bit of fire to it, so keep a cold drink within reach!

Makes 1 Loaf

1 cup yellow cornmeal

1 cup all-purpose flour

2 tablespoons sugar

1 tablespoon baking powder

1 teaspoon salt

½ teaspoon baking soda

¾ cup buttermilk

3 eggs

¼ cup butter, melted and cooled

1 cup shredded sharp cheddar cheese

1 can (4 oz.) diced jalapeño peppers

Preheat oven to 450°. Spray an 8-inch square baking dish with nonstick cooking spray.

1 In a large bowl, mix together cornmeal, flour, sugar, baking powder, salt and baking soda. Stir well to mix.

2 In another bowl, mix together buttermilk, eggs, butter, cheese and jalapeño peppers.

3 Pour buttermilk mixture into cornmeal-flour mixture and stir only until combined; do not overmix.

4 Pour batter into prepared baking dish. Place in oven and bake for 20 minutes. Remove to a cooling rack. Let cornbread sit for 5 minutes, turn over and remove from dish. Serve warm.

Green Chile Cornbread
Use 1 can (4 oz.) mild green chiles instead of the jalapeños in step 2.

Spicy Chile Cornbread
Use a combination of both mild green chiles and jalapeños that equal ½ cup in step 2.

Bacon and Jalapeño Cornbread
Add in ½ cup cooked crumbled bacon in step 2.

Egg Bread

Egg bread turns French toast into a morning treat. The golden color and gentle flavor make this a good bread for any occasion.

Makes 2 Loaves

1 pkg. active dry yeast

¼ cup warm water (110°)

1 cup warm milk (110°)

3 eggs

½ cup vegetable oil

2 teaspoons salt

¼ cup sugar

5½ cups bread flour

1 In a large bowl, dissolve yeast in warm water. In another bowl, combine warm milk, eggs and oil. Mix together well. Add to dissolved yeast.

2 Add in salt, sugar and bread flour, stirring to make a soft dough. Turn dough out onto a lightly floured surface and knead until smooth, about 5 minutes.

3 Lightly oil a large bowl. Place dough in bowl and turn over once to coat dough with oil. Cover and let rise in a warm place until double, about 1 hour.

4 Punch dough down. Place dough on a work surface and let rest for 10 minutes.

5 Cut dough in half and shape each half into a loaf. Spray two 9-inch loaf pans with cooking spray. Place each loaf into a pan. Cover loaves and let rise until double in size, about 45 minutes.

6 Preheat oven to 350°. Bake loaves until the tops are brown and loaves sound hollow when tapped, about 40 minutes. Remove from oven and let cool in pan for 5 minutes; turn loaves out onto a cooling rack.

Raisin Egg Bread
Add 2 cups raisins in step 3.

Honey Egg Bread
Omit sugar and add ¼ cup honey in step 2.

Oatmeal Honey Bread

Oatmeal gives this loaf a bit of texture. It's especially good topped with jam or flavored butter. Make extra and save the leftovers for French toast.

Makes 1 Loaf

1 cup
warm water
(105°-115°)

1 pkg.
active dry yeast

¼ cup honey

2 teaspoons
butter, melted

1 teaspoon salt

½ cup quick-
cooking oats

2½ - 2¾ cups
bread flour

1 Pour ¼ cup warm water into a large bowl. Sprinkle yeast over water and let stand for 5 minutes. Stir to dissolve yeast.

2 Add remaining water, honey, melted butter, salt, oats and 1 cup of the bread flour. Using a mixer at low speed, beat ingredients until just mixed. Increase speed to medium and add ½ cup flour to make a thick batter. Stir in enough additional flour (by hand) to make a stiff dough that leaves the sides of the bowl.

3 Cover bowl loosely with a towel and set in a warm place to rise until double in size, about 1 hour.

4 Punch dough down. Grease bottom and sides of a 2-quart round casserole. Shape dough into a ball and place in prepared dish. Cover loosely with a towel and let rise until double in size, about 30 to 45 minutes.

5 Preheat oven to 350°. Place bread in oven and bake for about 40 minutes or until the bread sounds hollow when tapped. Remove bread from oven and immediately remove bread from casserole dish to a wire rack to cool.

Oatmeal Maple Bread
Omit honey and use ¼ cup pure maple syrup in step 2.

Rosemary and Garlic Focaccia

This bread makes great sandwiches; try it with prosciutto, provolone and tomato. In yeast breads, use raw garlic only for a topping as it might retard yeast growth.

Makes 1 Focaccia

1 pkg.
active dry yeast

¼ cup warm water
(110°)

1¼ cups warm milk

½ cup olive oil

3 - 3½ cups
bread flour

1 cup fine
semolina flour

1 teaspoon salt

1 tablespoon minced
fresh rosemary

3 cloves garlic,
minced

1   In a large bowl, sprinkle yeast over warm water and let stand for 5 minutes. Stir to dissolve yeast. Add milk, 6 tablespoons of the olive oil, 3 cups bread flour, semolina flour and salt. Stir to make a soft dough.

2   Transfer dough to a floured surface and knead until smooth and elastic, adding more flour if needed. Place dough in a large oiled bowl and turn to coat all sides with oil. Cover loosely with a towel and set in a warm place until doubled in size, about 1½ hours.

3   Punch down dough and transfer to a lightly floured work surface. Sprinkle rosemary over dough and knead lightly. Oil a 15-x-10-inch jelly roll pan. Gently spread dough to fit pan and cover dough loosely with a towel. Let dough rise until doubled in size, about 30 minutes.

4   Preheat oven to 350°. With your fingers, lightly dimple dough and brush with remaining 2 tablespoons olive oil. Sprinkle with garlic. Bake focaccia for about 20 to 25 minutes until lightly golden brown on top. Remove from oven and cool for 20 minutes before cutting.

Pine Nut and Parmesan Focaccia
Substitute ½ cup shredded Parmesan cheese and ½ cup pine nuts for rosemary in step 3. Omit garlic in step 4.

Sun-Dried Tomato and Garlic Focaccia
Substitute ¼ cup minced sun-dried tomatoes for rosemary in step 3.

Rustic Bread

This soft, chewy bread is great for dipping into the *Olive Oil Dipping Sauce* on page 27. If the bread gets stale, you can make crunchy croutons from the leftovers.

Makes 2 Loaves

1 pkg. active dry yeast

2 cups warm water (105°-115°)

1 teaspoon sugar

1 teaspoon salt

5 cups bread flour

1 In a large bowl, sprinkle yeast over 1/2 cup of the warm water and let stand for 5 minutes. Stir to dissolve yeast. Add remaining 1 1/2 cups water, sugar, salt and bread flour. With a mixer, stir to make a soft, sticky dough. (Dough will be sticky, not smooth.) Mix at low speed until flour is thoroughly incorporated.

2 Place dough in a large oiled bowl and turn to coat all sides with oil. Cover loosely with a towel and set in a warm place to rise until double in size, about 1 1/2 hours.

3 Punch dough down. Transfer dough to a lightly floured work surface and knead lightly to eliminate air bubbles. Cut dough into 2 pieces. With floured hands, shape each piece into a 12-inch log. Place logs on a baking sheet a few inches apart and cover loosely with a towel. Let rise for 30 minutes.

4 Preheat oven to 400°. Bake bread for about 40 minutes, until it sounds hollow when tapped. Cool on a rack.

Rustic Bread with Olives
Add 1 cup coarsely chopped kalamata or other brine-cured olives in step 3 (as you knead out the air bubbles). Knead only enough to incorporate olives.

Rustic Bread with Walnuts
Add 1 cup chopped walnuts in step 3 (as you knead out the air bubbles). Knead only enough to incorporate nuts.

Potato and Sausage Frittata

Frittatas are perfect for brunches and light suppers and go nicely with a tossed green salad.

Servings: 8

6 oz. pork breakfast sausage

1 tablespoon olive oil

1½ cups cubed red-skinned potato (about 1 large potato)

2 medium zucchini, cut into ½-inch cubes

8 eggs

¼ cup shredded Parmesan cheese

¼ teaspoon ground black pepper

Preheat oven to 350°. Spray an 8-x-8-inch baking dish with nonstick cooking spray.

1 In a medium skillet over medium-high heat, crumble sausage. Cook until done, but not brown. Remove from skillet and drain on paper towels. Discard any fat.

2 Add olive oil to skillet. Add potato and cook until potato just begins to brown, about 10 minutes. Remove potato from skillet and set aside.

3 Add zucchini to skillet and sauté until it just begins to soften, about 5 minutes. Remove from heat.

4 Spread potatoes evenly on the bottom of prepared baking dish. Place cooked sausage evenly over potatoes. Top sausage with cooked zucchini.

5 In a medium bowl, combine eggs, Parmesan and pepper. Mix well and pour over vegetable-meat mixture in baking dish. Bake frittata for 20 to 25 minutes or just until center is set. Serve immediately.

Potato and Zucchini Frittata
Omit sausage from steps 1 and 4.

Potato, Sausage and Onion Frittata
Substitute 1 chopped yellow onion, sautéed in olive oil until translucent, for zucchini in step 3 and 4. Layer cooked onions on top of sausage in step 4.

Breads & Breakfasts

23

Summer Frittata

For this frittata, use any type of vegetable that is ready for harvest from your summer garden. Customize it even more by snipping some of your favorite fresh herbs and adding them to the mix.

Servings: 8

2 tablespoons olive oil

1 yellow onion, chopped

6 medium zucchini, cut into small chunks

4 large tomatoes, cut into small chunks

8 eggs

⅓ cup shredded Parmesan cheese

¼ teaspoon freshly ground pepper

Preheat oven to 350°. Spray a 10-x-13-inch baking dish with nonstick cooking spray.

1   In a large skillet, heat olive oil over medium-high heat. Add chopped onion and sauté until onion begins to brown, about 8 minutes. Stir in zucchini and cook for 4 minutes. Allow to cool to room temperature. Add tomatoes and stir gently to mix.

2   In a large bowl, beat eggs until smooth. Add Parmesan and pepper and stir until thoroughly combined. Gently fold in tomatoes and zucchini-onion mixture.

3   Pour mixture into prepared dish. Bake for 45 to 60 minutes or until firm. Serve immediately or cool and serve at room temperature.

Artichoke Frittata
Omit zucchini and use 3 cups chopped artichoke hearts in steps 1 and 2.

Summer Frittata with Ricotta
In step 2, add 1 lb. ricotta cheese to beaten eggs.

Sour Cream Quiche

This quiche is a bit firmer than regular cream quiches. It holds up well to the addition of vegetables, meats or other variations.

Servings: 6~8

10 slices bacon, cooked and crumbled

4 eggs

2 cups sour cream

1/2 teaspoon salt

1/4 teaspoon freshly ground nutmeg

1 1/4 cups shredded Swiss cheese

one 9-inch deep-dish pie pastry

Preheat oven to 425°.

1 In a large bowl, combine bacon, eggs, sour cream, salt, nutmeg and cheese; stir to mix well.

2 Line a 9-inch pie pan with pastry and pour egg mixture into pan.

3 Bake for 15 minutes. Reduce oven heat to 350° and bake for an additional 45 minutes, until golden brown.

4 Remove from oven. Let stand at room temperature for 10 minutes before serving.

Cheddar and Bacon Quiche
Substitute cheddar cheese for Swiss cheese in step 1. Omit nutmeg.

Mexican Quiche
Substitute pepper Jack cheese for Swiss cheese in step 1. Omit bacon and nutmeg in step 1 and add 1 can (4 oz.) chopped mild green chiles.

Broccoli Quiche
Add 1 cup chopped raw broccoli in step 1. Omit nutmeg.

Spinach Quiche
Add 1 pkg.(10 oz.) frozen chopped spinach (squeezed dry) in step 1.

Appetizers

Appetizers

Olive Oil Dipping Sauce 30
Basil Olive Oil Dipping Sauce
Garlic Olive Oil Dipping Sauce
Fiery Olive Oil Dipping Sauce
Mixed Herb Olive Oil Dipping Sauce
Red Wine and Olive Oil Dipping Sauce

Mozzarella Cheese Bites 31
Basil Mozzarella Cheese Bites
Provence Herbed Cheese Bite

Pesto Palmiers 32
Sun-Dried Tomato Pesto Palmiers
Parmesan Palmiers

Olivada Spread 33
Green Olivada Spread
Rosemary Olivada Spread

Pork Pillows 34
Pork Spring Pillows
Shrimp Pillows

Sausage Polenta Squares 35
Cheese and Prosciutto Polenta Squares
Sweet Red Pepper Polenta Squares

Spinach-Stuffed Portobello Mushrooms 36
Sausage-Stuffed Portobello Mushrooms
Cheese-Stuffed Portobello Mushrooms

Grilled Quesadillas with Salsa Cruda 37
Grilled Crab Quesadillas
Grilled Chicken Quesadillas

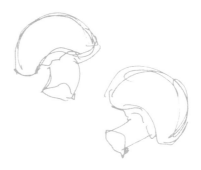

Rosemary Chicken Skewers 38
Lemon Rosemary Chicken Skewers
Basil Rosemary Chicken Skewers
Tarragon Chicken Skewers
Rosemary Pork Skewers

Lemon-Herb Shrimp 40
Lemon-Basil Shrimp
Lemon-Herb Scallops
Lemon-Herb Crab Legs

Shrimp with Lemon Aioli 41
Shrimp with Lemon-Caper Aioli
Shrimp with Lemon-Peppercorn Ailoi

Poached Salmon with Sweet Red Pepper Vinaigrette 42
Poached Salmon with Shallot-Chive Vinaigrette
Poached Salmon with Dill-Scallion Vinaigrette

Classic Crab Cakes 44
Classic Shrimp Cakes
Classic Salmon Cakes

Olive Oil Dipping Sauce

Use one of these dippers as a substitute for butter at your next meal. Not only is olive oil more flavorful, but it is also more healthful.

Makes 1 1/4 Cups

1 cup high-grade olive oil

1 teaspoon dried oregano

1 clove garlic, minced

1/4 teaspoon freshly ground black pepper

2 tablespoons balsamic vinegar

1 In a small container, combine all ingredients. Let flavors blend for a minimum of 3 hours. Mix well and pour on a shallow plate.

Basil Olive Oil Dipping Sauce
Use 1 teaspoon dried basil instead of oregano

Garlic Olive Oil Dipping Sauce
Use 2 cloves garlic instead of just 1.

Fiery Olive Oil Dipping Sauce
Add 1/4 teaspoon dried red chile peppers.

Mixed Herb Olive Oil Dipping Sauce
Add 1 tablespoon minced fresh chives.

Red Wine and Olive Oil Dipping Sauce
Omit balsamic vinegar and add 1 tablespoon red wine vinegar.

Mozzarella Cheese Bites

These herbed cheese treats are the perfect appetizer to serve with wine. Serve them with thinly sliced French baguettes, fresh seedless red or green grapes and other cheeses for your next gathering.

Servings: 4~6

2 tablespoons minced fresh chives

2 tablespoons minced fresh Italian parsley

2 cloves garlic, minced

1/4 cup olive oil

2 tablespoons apple cider vinegar

1/4 teaspoon salt

1/4 teaspoon pepper

8 oz. mozzarella cheese, cut into 1-inch cubes

sliced French baguette for serving

1 In a medium bowl, combine chives, parsley, garlic, olive oil, vinegar, salt and pepper and stir to combine.

2 Add mozzarella cheese and stir to mix. Cover and refrigerate for at least 3 hours.

3 Place on a serving dish and serve with sliced baguettes.

Basil Mozzarella Cheese Bites
Substitute 2 tablespoons minced fresh basil for Italian parsley in step 1.

Provence Herbed Cheese Bites
Substitute 2 tablespoons minced fresh chervil for Italian parsley in step 1.

Pesto Palmiers

These appetizers are also addicting. You can assemble them early in the day and pop them into the oven when guests arrive.

Servings: 4-6

2 sheets frozen puff pastry, thawed

2/3 cup prepared basil pesto

Spray a baking sheet with nonstick cooking spray.

1 Lay one pastry sheet flat on a work surface. Spread 1/3 cup of the pesto evenly over pastry.

2 Starting from one short side, roll up jelly roll-style to center. Starting at the second short side, roll up to the center. Press two sides together and wrap in plastic wrap. Place in refrigerator to chill for 1 hour. Repeat with other pastry sheet and remaining pesto.

3 Preheat oven to 400°. Remove pastry from plastic wrap. Slice into 1/2-inch-thick slices and arrange on baking sheet, cut side down and spacing 1 inch apart.

4 Bake for about 20 minutes or until golden brown. Serve warm.

Sun-Dried Tomato Pesto Palmiers
Omit basil pesto and use 2/3 cup sun-dried tomato pesto instead in step 1.

Parmesan Palmiers
Omit basil pesto and use 1/2 cup shredded Parmesan cheese in step 1.

Olivada Spread

Usually served with sliced baguettes, this spread can also be rubbed on chicken before roasting for a Tucsan-style chicken dinner.

Makes 1 Cup

1 teaspoon
olive oil

1 anchovy fillet

1 clove garlic

1 cup pitted
kalamata olives

1 With a blender or food processor, combine olive oil, anchovy and garlic. Pulse until a smooth paste.

2 Add olives and pulse until mixture is well chopped, but not smooth.

3 Place olivada mixture into a small container, cover and refrigerate for at least 4 hours. Serve with baguette slices.

Green Olivada Spread
Use 1 cup green olives (pimiento-stuffed olives) to replace of the kalamata olives in step 2.

Rosemary Olivada Spread
Add 1 teaspoon fresh rosemary in step 1.

Pork Pillows

The shape of these Asian-style dumplings resemble small pillows. Their handy size will work well as an appetizer at your next dinner party.

Servings: 8

1 lb. ground pork

1 egg

1 clove garlic, minced

1 tablespoon soy sauce

2 teaspoons ground ginger

1/4 teaspoon salt

1/2 teaspoon sesame oil

1/4 cup chopped fresh cilantro

3 tablespoons slivered green onions

2 tablespoons cornstarch

2 tablespoons water

1 pkg. 2-inch square won ton wrappers

vegetable shortening for deep-frying

1 In a medium skillet, crumble ground pork and cook over medium-high heat until cooked through, about 10 minutes. Drain fat and cool.

2 In a medium bowl, combine egg, garlic, soy sauce, ginger, salt and sesame oil and stir to mix well. Add pork, cilantro and green onion and stir to mix.

3 To assemble pillows, dissolve cornstarch in water. Place a won ton wrapper on a work surface and brush edges with cornstarch mixture. Place 1 heaping tablespoon of the pork mixture onto center of wrapper. Top meat mixture with another won ton wrapper and press edges together to resemble a stuffed pillow. Repeat with remaining filling and won ton wrappers.

4 Heat shortening in a wok or a deep saucepan. Place a few pillows in hot shortening, being careful not to over-crowd or have pillows touch each other. Deep-fry until golden brown, about 3 to 5 minutes. Remove from shortening with a slotted spoon and drain on paper towels. Serve hot.

Pork Spring Pillows
Add 1/2 cup shredded carrots and 1/2 cup shredded cabbage in step 2.

Shrimp Pillows
Omit pork and use 1 lb. shrimp meat in step 2.

Sausage Polenta Squares

When cooked polenta cools it becomes very firm and can be sliced into serving pieces. The slices are solid enough to stand up to a heavy topping and make perfect appetizers.

Servings: 4~6

Sauce
1/2 lb. Italian sausage, casings removed

1/2 yellow onion, minced

1 can (8 oz.) tomato sauce

1/2 cup red wine or beef broth

1/4 teaspoon dried oregano

1/4 teaspoon dried basil

1/4 teaspoon salt

1 teaspoon sugar

polenta, page 80

olive oil

1 Crumble sausage into a large skillet. Sauté sausage over high heat until beginning to brown; drain fat.

2 Add onion, reduce heat to medium and sauté until onion is translucent. Add tomato sauce, red wine or broth, oregano, basil, salt and sugar and bring mixture to a boil. Reduce heat to low and simmer for 25 to 30 minutes or until mixture is thickened. Keep warm.

3 Heat broiler. Slice cooked polenta into 1/2-inch-thick slices, about 2 inches square. Place polenta squares on a very lightly oiled baking sheet and brush tops with a small amount of olive oil. Broil for 5 to 8 minutes per side or until lightly browned. Place on paper towels to drain.

4 Place 1 tablespoon of the sausage mixture on each polenta square and serve immediately.

Cheese and Prosciutto Polenta Squares

Omit sauce. Start recipe from step 3. In step 4, top each polenta square with a slice of prosciutto (about 4 oz. total) and about 1 tablespoon shredded mozzarella cheese (about 1 cup total). Return polenta squares to baking sheet and broil for an additional 3 to 5 minutes or until cheese is melted. Serve immediately.

Sweet Red Pepper Polenta Squares

Omit sausage. Start recipe from step 2 and add 2 tablespoons butter in place of sausage fat. Add 1 cup chopped red bell peppers and sauté with onion.

Spinach~Stuffed Portobello Mushrooms

Portobello mushrooms are large and meaty. Their wide surface can hold all types of stuffings. Serve them as appetizers or as an unexpected side dish.

Servings: 4

1 pkg. (10 oz.) frozen chopped spinach

2 eggs

1/3 cup minced yellow onion

1 clove garlic, minced

1/4 teaspoon salt

1/4 cup grated Parmesan cheese

1/4 teaspoon freshly ground nutmeg

1/2 cup fresh breadcrumbs

2 portobello mushrooms, 4 to 5 inches in diameter

Preheat oven to 450°.

1 In a large bowl, combine all ingredients except mushrooms. Stir to mix thoroughly.

2 Remove stems from mushrooms. Rinse and dry mushrooms.

3 Divide spinach mixture in half. Gently mound 1/2 of the spinach mixture on the underside of one mushroom. Mound remaining spinach mixture on other mushroom cap.

4 Place mushrooms on an ungreased baking sheet. Place in oven and bake for about 20 to 25 minutes.

5 Cool for a few minutes. Cut into wedges and serve.

Sausage~Stuffed Portobello Mushrooms
Use only 1/2 pkg. spinach and add 1/3 cup cooked, crumbled Italian sausage in step 1.

Cheese~Stuffed Portobello Mushrooms
Use 1 cup ricotta cheese in place of the spinach in step 1. Increase Parmesan cheese to 1/2 cup.

Grilled Quesadillas with Salsa Cruda

This is a great appetizer to nibble on while you are barbecuing a meal. Try using some of the flavored tortillas that are now on the market, such as spinach, tomato or chile.

Servings: 4

Salsa Cruda
2 cups chopped tomatoes

1/4 cup minced red onion

1/4 cup chopped fresh cilantro

1/4 teaspoon ground cumin

1/4 teaspoon salt

Quesadillas
4 flour tortillas, about 10 inches in diameter

1 cup shredded pepper Jack cheese

1/2 cup shredded fresh spinach leaves

Prepare a medium-hot grill.

1 For salsa, combine all ingredients in a medium bowl. Let stand for 10 minutes before serving to allow flavors to blend.

2 Place 2 tortillas on a flat work surface. On each tortilla, sprinkle 1/2 cup shredded cheese. Keep cheese within 1 inch of the edge. Scatter 1/4 cup spinach over cheese and top remaining tortillas.

3 Place quesadillas on preheated grill. Cook for about 2 minutes, carefully flip and continue grilling for an additional 2 minutes. The tortillas should be lightly browned on each side.

4 Remove from grill and cut each quesadilla into quarters. Serve immediately and garnish with *Salsa Cruda*.

Grilled Crab Quesadillas
Omit spinach. Use 1/2 cup flaked crabmeat over each tortilla in place of the spinach in step 2.

Grilled Chicken Quesadillas
Omit spinach. Use 1/2 cup cooked chicken over each tortilla in place of the spinach in step 2.

Rosemary Chicken Skewers

These can be served as an appetizer or main dish. Try a bottle of crisp Chardonnay; it mingles well with the herbs and garlic.

Servings: 6~8

4 boneless, skinless chicken breasts, cut into 2-inch chunks

1 clove garlic, minced

¼ teaspoon freshly ground black pepper

1 teaspoon chopped fresh rosemary

¼ cup dry white wine

Sauce
¼ cup butter

½ teaspoon chopped fresh rosemary

1 clove garlic, minced

2 tablespoons dry white wine

¼ teaspoon salt

8 metal skewers or bamboo skewers

If using bamboo skewers, soak them in water for 30 minutes.

1 In a medium bowl, combine chicken, garlic, pepper, rosemary and ¼ cup white wine; toss to coat. Cover bowl and marinate for 4 hours in the refrigerator or ½ hour at room temperature.

2 Prepare a medium-hot barbecue fire. Thread chicken on skewers, using about ½ breast per skewer.

3 Grill chicken until just done, about 10 minutes, turning frequently and basting with remaining marinade.

4 Combine sauce ingredients in a small saucepan. Bring to a boil over medium heat; remove from heat.

5 Place chicken skewers on a serving plate and drizzle with sauce. Serve immediately.

Lemon Rosemary Chicken Skewers

Use 2 tablespoons lemon juice instead of the white wine for the sauce in step 4.

Basil Rosemary Chicken Skewers

Use fresh basil instead of rosemary in the marinade and sauce in steps 1 and 4.

Tarragon Chicken Skewers

Use fresh tarragon instead of the rosemary in marinade and sauce in steps 1 and 4.

Rosemary Pork Skewers

Use 1 lb. pork loin instead of chicken breasts in step 1.

Lemon~Herb Shrimp

You can skewer the shrimp and mix up the sauce early in the day, as long as you keep them tightly wrapped. Pour the sauce over the shrimp when you are ready to serve.

Servings: 6~8

2 tablespoons minced fresh chives

2 tablespoons finely chopped fresh parsley

juice of 2 lemons

grated zest of 1 lemon

1 tablespoon Dijon-style mustard

¼ cup olive oil

2 tablespoons vegetable oil

¼ teaspoon freshly ground black pepper

¼ teaspoon salt

2 lb. large shrimp, cooked

1 In a medium bowl, combine chives, parsley, lemon juice, lemon zest, mustard, olive oil, vegetable oil, pepper and salt. Stir to mix well.

2 Add shrimp to bowl and stir to coat all shrimp evenly with marinade.

3 Thread 3 or 4 shrimp onto a bamboo skewer and serve immediately.

Lemon~Basil Shrimp
Substitute 2 tablespoons chopped fresh basil for parsley in step 1.

Lemon~Herb Scallops
Substitute 2 lb. cooked sea scallops for shrimp in steps 2 and 3.

Lemon~Herb Crab Legs
In step 1, transfer lemon-herb mixture to a small serving bowl. In step 2, substitute 4 lb. cooked crab legs for shrimp and do not add crab legs to lemon-herb mixture. Serve crab legs on a platter with lemon-herb mixture for dipping.

Shrimp with Lemon Aioli

Aioli is a rich mayonnaise-like dipping sauce that goes wonderfully with seafood. Lemon zest and lemon juice make a perfect accompaniment to a shrimp appetizer.

Servings: 6~8

8 cloves garlic

juice and grated zest of 1 lemon

2 egg yolks

½ cup vegetable oil

½ cup olive oil

1½ lb. large shrimp, cooked

1 In a blender container, combine garlic cloves, lemon juice, zest and egg yolks. Pulse until smooth and light yellow in color.

2 Combine vegetable oil and olive oil. Turn blender on high and slowly pour oil in a steady stream; gradually increase the amount of oil poured as the mixture thickens. Do not let oil pool.

3 Remove aioli from blender and place in a bowl with a tight-fitting lid. Refrigerate for 3 to 4 hours to let flavors blend. Keep refrigerated until ready to use.

4 Place shrimp on a serving platter and serve with aioli.

Shrimp with Lemon~Caper Aioli
Add 2 tablespoons drained and rinsed capers to the aïoli in step 3. Stir to mix in capers well.

Shrimp with Lemon~Peppercorn Aioli
Add 2 tablespoons drained and rinsed green peppercorns to the aioli in step 3. Stir to mix in the green peppercorns well.

Poached Salmon with Sweet Red Pepper Vinaigrette

This can be served as a buffet appetizer, a first course or a light summer entrée. The red color of the bell pepper dressing complements the pink of the salmon and makes a lovely presentation.

Servings: 8~10

1 salmon fillet, 3 to 4 lb.

1/2 cup cider vinegar

1/2 cup minced red bell pepper

3 tablespoons capers, rinsed

1 clove garlic, minced

1/2 teaspoon salt

1 Place salmon in a large poaching rack or steamer. Add water to pan until water level is about 1/2 inch below top of fish. Bring water to a boil over high heat. Reduce heat to low, cover and simmer for 20 to 30 minutes, or until salmon flakes easily when tested with a fork.

2 Transfer salmon to a serving platter. Cover with plastic wrap and refrigerate until well chilled.

3 In a small bowl, combine vinegar, bell pepper, capers, garlic and salt. Cover and refrigerate for at least 30 minutes to blend flavors. To serve, spoon vinaigrette over salmon.

Poached Salmon with Shallot~Chive Vinaigrette

Omit red peppers and capers from step 3. Add 1/4 cup minced shallots and 1/4 cup minced chives.

Poached Salmon with Dill~Scallion Vinaigrette

Omit red peppers and capers from step 3. Add 1/4 cup minced scallions and 1 tablespoon fresh chopped dill.

salmon

Classic Crab Cakes

You can make these crab cakes as appetizers, a main course or even as an addition to a salad. To make them as appetizers or for a salad, shape them into patties about 1 inch in diameter.

Servings: 4

½ lb. cooked crabmeat

¾ cup fresh breadcrumbs

1 egg, beaten

2 tablespoons mayonnaise

¾ teaspoon Old Bay Seasoning

¼ teaspoon grated lemon zest

2 tablespoons butter

1 In a large bowl, combine crabmeat, breadcrumbs, egg, mayonnaise, Old Bay and lemon zest. Stir to mix well.

2 Form mixture into six ½-inch-thick patties.

3 Heat butter in a large skillet over medium heat. Add cakes and cook until golden brown, about 4 to 5 minutes per side. Remove from skillet and serve immediately.

Classic Shrimp Cakes
Omit crabmeat from step 1 and use 1/2 lb. cooked shrimp meat instead.

Classic Salmon Cakes
Omit crabmeat from step 1 and use 1/2 lb. cooked, flaked salmon instead.

Salads

Salads

Simply Perfect Salad 50
Simply Perfect Summer Salad
Simply Perfect Vegetable Salad

Artichoke and Tomato Salad 51
Tomato and Hearts of Palm Salad
Greek Artichoke and Tomato Salad

Grilled Vegetable Salad 52
Grilled Eggplant and Vegetable Salad
Herbed Grilled Vegetable Salad

Mediterranean Cobb Salad 53
Southwestern Cobb Salad
San Francisco Cobb Salad

Asian Noodle Salad 54
Thai-Peanut Noodle Salad
Asian Noodle Salad with Chicken

Greek-Style Couscous Salad 55
Greek-Style Couscous Salad
  with Sun-Dried Tomatoes
Italian-Style Couscous Salad

Caesar Tortellini Salad 56
Romaine and Tortellini Salad
Pasta Caesar Salad

Spinach and Bacon Salad 57
Spinach and Cheese Salad
Italian Spinach Salad

Cashew Chicken Salad 58
Almond Chicken Salad
Cashew Turkey Salad
Creamy Cashew Chicken Salad

Curried Chicken Salad 59
Curried Turkey Salad
Chicken and Potato Salad
Turkey and Potato Salad

Simply Perfect Salad

A tossed green salad with a light vinaigrette is simply a perfect accompaniment for any meal. This salad can be dressed up with different vegetables and lettuces.

Servings: 4

¾ cup
vegetable oil

⅓ cup
cider vinegar

1 tablespoon
Dijon-style mustard

1 clove garlic,
minced

¾ teaspoon salt

⅛ teaspoon freshly
ground black pepper

4 cups torn
romaine lettuce leaves

freshly grated
Parmesan cheese

1 In a small bowl, combine oil, vinegar, mustard, garlic, salt and pepper. Mix well and set aside.

2 In a large bowl, place romaine lettuce and drizzle dressing over greens to taste (you will have dressing left over. Store dressing in a covered container for up to 2 weeks in refrigerator). Toss to mix and serve. Sprinkle Parmesan cheese on top, if desired.

Simply Perfect Summer Salad
Thinly slice 4 large ripe beefsteak tomatoes and arrange slices on top of each salad plate. Drizzle a bit more dressing over tomatoes and serve.

Simply Perfect Vegetable Salad
Omit romaine lettuce and use 1 cup thinly sliced zucchini, 1 cup thinly sliced carrots, 1 cup thinly sliced green bell peppers and 1 cup thinly sliced sweet red onion in step 2.

Artichoke and Tomato Salad

Perfect for a special dinner or a casual picnic, this salad can be assembled early in the day and tossed with the dressing just before serving.

Servings: 4~6

1 cup canned
baby corn ears

4 cups coarsely
chopped tomatoes

2 jars (7.5 oz. each)
artichoke hearts,
coarsely chopped

½ cup slivered
green onions

1 cup olive oil

½ cup cider vinegar

½ teaspoon salt

grated zest
of 1 lemon

¼ teaspoon
dried oregano

¼ teaspoon
dried basil

¼ teaspoon
dried thyme

1 Cut baby corn into ½-inch thick slices. Place sliced corn in a large bowl. Add tomato, artichoke hearts and green onions; stir to mix.

2 In a medium bowl, combine remaining ingredients and stir well to mix. Pour dressing over artichoke and tomato mixture and toss well. Serve immediately.

Tomato and Hearts of Palm Salad
Use 2 cans (14 oz. each) hearts of palm (cut into ½ slices) in place of artichoke hearts in steps 1 and 2. Omit baby corn.

Greek Artichoke and Tomato Salad
Add ½ cup crumbled feta cheese and ½ cup pitted kalamata olives.

Grilled Vegetable Salad

More of a vegetable side dish than a true salad, this lively combination makes a lovely presentation.

Servings: 4-6

¼ cup olive oil

¼ teaspoon dried basil

¼ teaspoon freshly ground black pepper

3 medium zucchini

4 stalks celery

1 yellow onion

1 green bell pepper

2 tablespoons balsamic vinegar

1 tablespoon capers

¼ teaspoon salt

1 Early in the day, combine olive oil, basil and black pepper in a small container. Let stand at room temperature for at least 4 hours.

2 Prepare a medium-hot grill. Slice zucchini lengthwise into thirds. Cut celery stalks widthwise into thirds (about the same length as zucchini). Cut onion widthwise into 4 pieces about 1/2-inch thick. Stem and seed green pepper and cut lengthwise into quarters.

3 In a large, shallow bowl, combine seasoned oil and vegetables and toss gently to coat.

4 Grill vegetables until tender-crisp. Turn once: about 6 minutes for zucchini; for celery, onion and green pepper, about 2 minutes. Reserve seasoned oil. Transfer vegetables to a shallow bowl and cool to room temperature. Cut vegetables into bite-sized pieces.

5 In a small bowl, combine reserved oil, vinegar, capers and salt. Pour mixture over vegetables. Toss very gently with your hands to coat. Serve immediately.

Grilled Eggplant and Vegetable Salad
Substitute 1 medium eggplant for zucchini in step 3. Slice unpeeled eggplant into 1/2-inch-thick slices.

Herbed Grilled Vegetable Salad
Add 1/4 teaspoon dried oregano leaves and 1 clove garlic, minced, to seasoned oil in step 1.

Mediterranean Cobb Salad

This version of Cobb salad features a light balsamic vinaigrette, rather than the more traditional blue cheese or ranch dressing. Served with crusty French bread, it makes a terrific light summer meal.

Servings: 4-6

¼ cup balsamic vinegar

⅓ cup olive oil

¼ teaspoon salt

¼ teaspoon freshly ground black pepper

6 cups chopped romaine lettuce

4 hard-cooked eggs, peeled and chopped

¾ cup crumbled feta cheese

1 cup chopped cooked pancetta

1½ cups chopped tomatoes

½ cup pitted kalamata olives

½ cup roasted red bell peppers

pancetta: an unsmoked Italian bacon that is cured with salt and other spices. Look for it in an Italian deli or specialty food store.

1 In a small bowl, combine vinegar, olive oil, salt and pepper; set aside.

2 In a large bowl, place all chopped lettuce.

3 Place eggs, feta, pancetta, tomato, olives and roasted red peppers in separate rows on top of lettuce.

4 Pour blended dressing over salad. Toss salad to mix just before serving.

Southwestern Cobb Salad

Omit balsamic vinegar from step 1 and use 3 tbs. cider vinegar. Omit feta from step 3 and use ¾ cup shredded pepper Jack cheese. Omit pancetta from step 3 and use 1 cup sliced smoked chicken breast. Omit kalamata olive from step 3 and use ½ cup fresh corn kernels (or use ½ cup frozen cut corn that has been defrosted).

San Francisco Cobb Salad

Omit feta from step 3 and use ¾ cup shredded cheddar. Omit pancetta from step 3 and use 1 cup cooked crab meat. Omit kalamata olives and red peppers from step 3 and use 1 cup cubed avocado.

Asian Noodle Salad

This cold pasta salad can be made any time of year. Substitute a jar of roasted red peppers if fresh ones are not in season.

Servings: 4~6

1/4 cup
rice vinegar

1 tablespoon
sesame oil

1/2 cup
vegetable oil

1 teaspoon
soy sauce

1 clove garlic, minced

1 lb. fresh or dried
angel hair pasta

1 cup
shredded carrots

1/2 cup slivered
green onions

1/2 cup slivered
snow pea pods

3/4 cup thinly sliced
red bell peppers

1 In a small bowl, combine rice vinegar, sesame oil, vegetable oil, soy sauce and garlic. Stir to mix and set aside.

2 Cook pasta according to package directions. Rinse with cool water when cooked, drain and place pasta in a large bowl.

3 Add carrots, green onions, pea pods and red bell peppers to pasta.

4 Pour dressing over pasta and vegetables; toss to mix.

5 Serve at room temperature or refrigerate; serve chilled.

Thai~Peanut Noodle Salad
Add 2 tablespoons smooth peanut butter and 1 tsp. dried red chile pepper flakes in step 1.

Asian Noodle Salad with Chicken
Add 1 1/2 cups cooked chopped chicken in step 3.

Greek-Style Couscous Salad

Tiny grains of pasta called couscous cook quickly. All you need to do is pour boiling water over them and you have a tasty addition to any salad. Here couscous is livened up with components of a classic Greek salad.

Servings: 4

2 cups cooked
couscous, cooled

1/2 cup diced
cucumber

1/2 cup diced tomato

1/4 cup coarsely
chopped pitted
kalamata olives

2 tablespoons
crumbled feta
cheese

Dressing
2/3 cup olive oil

1/4 cup
red wine vinegar

1/4 teaspoon
dried oregano

1/8 teaspoon salt

1/8 teaspoon freshly
ground black pepper

1 In a medium bowl, combine cooked couscous, cucumber, tomatoes, olives and feta cheese.

2 In a separate bowl, combine all dressing ingredients; mix well.

3 Pour dressing over salad. Stir well to combine. Refrigerate until cold; serve.

Greek-Style Couscous Salad with Sun-Dried Tomatoes
In place of diced tomatoes, use 1/4 cup finely chopped sun-dried tomatoes in step 1.

Italian-Style Couscous Salad
In place of feta cheese, add 2 tablespoons shredded Parmesan cheese and add 1/4 cup pine nuts in step 1.

Caesar Tortellini Salad

The bright flavors of a Caesar salad make an interesting dressing for this pasta salad. Use more garlic or anchovies if you are feeling adventurous.

Servings: 4~6

3 cloves garlic

½ cup olive oil

3 tablespoons fresh lemon juice

1 teaspoon grated lemon zest

6 anchovies

1 lb. fresh or frozen tortellini

¼ cup freshly grated Parmesan cheese

1 Combine garlic, olive oil, lemon juice, lemon zest and anchovies in a blender container. Pulse until smooth; set aside.

2 Cook tortellini according to package instructions. When done, rinse in cold water to cool; drain well.

3 In a large bowl, combine cooked tortellini and dressing. Toss to mix. Sprinkle Parmesan over pasta and toss again. Serve immediately.

Romaine and Tortellini Salad
Place completed salad on top of 4 cups torn romaine lettuce.

Pasta Caesar Salad
Use 1 pound of any pasta shape in place of tortellini in step 2 and 3.

Spinach and Bacon Salad

This version of a classic spinach salad features lots of surprise ingredients to keep each bite interesting.

Servings: 4

4 cups fresh spinach leaves, well-washed and dried

1 hard-cooked egg, peeled and sliced

⅓ cup sliced sweet red onion

½ cup sliced white mushrooms

2 tablespoons cooked, crumbled bacon

Dressing
¼ cup olive oil

1 tablespoon red wine vinegar

1½ tablespoons balsamic vinegar

1 In a large bowl, combine all salad ingredients.

2 In a separate small bowl, combine dressing ingredients; stir to mix.

3 Drizzle dressing over salad ingredients, toss to coat and serve immediately.

Spinach and Cheese Salad
Add ¼ cup shredded Swiss cheese in step 1.

Italian Spinach Salad
Add ¼ cup shredded Parmesan in step 1. Use ¼ cup minced, cooked pancetta in place of bacon in step 1.

Cashew Chicken Salad

All the ingredients you love in a Chinese-style cashew chicken entrée are disguised as a light salad. It's great served over shredded lettuce.

Servings: 4-6

4 boneless, skinless chicken breast halves, cooked and chopped

1/2 cup cashew pieces

1/2 cup shredded peeled carrots

1/4 cup slivered green onions

1/2 cup coarsely chopped water chestnuts

Dressing
1/2 cup rice vinegar

1/2 cup vegetable oil

1/2 teaspoon sesame oil

1/2 teaspoon ground ginger

1/2 teaspoon salt

1 In a large bowl, combine chicken, cashews, carrots, green onions and water chestnuts. Stir to mix; set aside.

2 In a small bowl, combine all dressing ingredients; stir well to mix.

3 Pour dressing over chicken mixture and stir well to mix. Serve over shredded lettuce.

Almond Chicken Salad
Omit cashews and use 1/2 cup slivered almonds in step 1.

Cashew Turkey Salad
Omit chicken and use 1 large cooked turkey breast in step 1. Remove skin from cooked breast and chop.

Creamy Cashew Chicken Salad
Omit vinegar and oil from dressing and use 1 cup mayonnaise in step 2. Increase ginger to 3/4 teaspoon in step 2.

Curried Chicken Salad

This salad uses just a touch of curry powder to lend full flavor without the spiciness found in most curry dishes. It is a very filling salad, suitable for a luncheon entrée. It also makes a great filling for sandwiches.

Servings: 4

2 medium-sized red potatoes, unpeeled

2 skinless chicken breast halves, cooked and chopped

1/2 cup chopped celery

3 tablespoons minced green onions

2/3 cup raisins

1 1/3 cups mayonnaise

3 tablespoons red wine vinegar

1/2 teaspoon salt

5 teaspoons curry powder

1 Scrub potatoes and place in a small pot. Add water to cover potatoes and cook on high heat until boiling. Reduce heat to medium and cook until potatoes are tender, about 20 minutes. Drain potatoes and cool.

2 In a medium bowl, cut potatoes into 1/2-inch cubes. Add chicken, celery, onions and raisins.

3 In another small bowl, combine mayonnaise, vinegar, salt and curry powder. Stir to mix well; add to chicken mixture. Stir well, cover and refrigerate until chilled. Serve in sandwiches or on lettuce.

Curried Turkey Salad
Omit chicken breasts and use 1 cooked skinless turkey breast (about 3 cups chopped turkey) in step 2.

Chicken and Potato Salad
Omit raisins from step 2 and curry powder from step 3.

Turkey and Potato Salad
Omit chicken breasts and use 1 cooked skinless turkey breast (about 3 cups chopped turkey) in step 2. Omit raisins from step 2 and curry powder from step 3.

Soups

Soups

Fresh Tomato Soup 64
Fresh Tomato and Basil Soup
Fresh Tomato and Leek Soup
Fresh Heirloom Tomato Soup

Gazpacho 65
Blended Gazpacho
Crab Gazpacho
Shrimp Gazpacho

Asian Vegetable Soup 66
Asian Vegetable Soup with Tofu
Asian Vegetable Soup with Shrimp

Autumn Soup 67
Autumn Honey and Pumpkin Soup
Winter Vegetable Soup
Spring Vegetable Soup

Butternut Squash Soup 68
Apple Butternut Squash Soup
Butternut Squash Soup (low-fat)
Curried Butternut Squash Soup

Golden Mushroom Soup 69
Mixed Mushroom Soup
Golden Mushroom and Potato Soup

Cream of Artichoke Soup 70
Cream of Broccoli Soup
Cream of Asparagus Soup
Cream of Carrot Soup

Fiery Cream of Red Pepper Soup 71
Fiery Cream of Yellow Pepper Soup
Cream of Roasted Red Pepper Soup

Roasted Corn Chowder 72

Fresh Corn Chowder
Smoky Roasted Corn Chowder
Spring Vegetable and Roasted Corn
  Chowder
Roasted Corn and Red Pepper Chowder

Black Bean Soup with Sausage 74

Black Bean Soup with Ham
Arizona Black Bean Soup

Italian Meatball Soup 75

Italian Meatball and Tortellini Soup
Italian Tortellini Soup

Shrimp Bisque 76

Crab Bisque
Lobster Bisque
Seafod Bisque

Fresh Tomato Soup

This is the perfect soup to make in late summer when gardens are abundant with tomatoes. Once you see how easy it is to make fresh tomato soup, you will never want to eat soup from a can again.

Servings: 4

¼ cup butter

1 yellow onion, chopped

4 cups chopped fresh tomatoes

¼ teaspoon freshly ground black pepper

½ teaspoon salt

½ cup chicken broth

1 In a large soup pot, melt butter over medium-high heat. Add onion and sauté until onion just begins to brown.

2 Add tomato, pepper, salt and chicken broth. Bring mixture to a boil; cover and reduce heat to low. Simmer for 20 minutes.

3 Pour soup (in batches if necessary) into a blender container or process with a food processor. Pulse until smooth. Return soup to pot and heat to boiling. Serve immediately.

Fresh Tomato and Basil Soup
After pureeing soup in step 3, add ¼ cup finely chopped fresh basil and bring to a boil. Serve immediately.

Fresh Tomato and Leek Soup
Omit onion from step 1 and thinly slice 2 large leeks to use in place of the onion.

Fresh Heirloom Tomato Soup
Use 4 cups yellow plum tomatoes (or other heirloom tomato) in place of tomatoes in step 2.

Gazpacho

A simple Spanish-style chilled soup called gazpacho has hundreds of variations. It makes a perfect summer meal on a hot day or serve with some chips, guacamole and a pitcher of sangria.

Servings: 4

1 cup
chopped celery

1 cup chopped
peeled cucumbers

2/3 cup chopped
red onion

2 cups chopped
tomatoes

1 cup chopped
green bell peppers

1 teaspoon
ground cumin

1/2 teaspoon freshly
ground black pepper

1/2 teaspoon salt

3 cups vegetable
juice, such as V-8

1 In a large bowl, combine all ingredients, stirring well to mix. Refrigerate for 30 minutes and serve cold.

Blended Gazpacho
After combining ingredients in step 1, pour soup into a blender container and pulse until vegetables are finely chopped (the soup should not be smooth). Refrigerate and serve chilled.

Crab Gazpacho
Just before serving, add 1 cup cooked crabmeat to soup.

Shrimp Gazpacho
Just before serving, add 1 cup cooked shrimp meat to soup.

Asian Vegetable Soup

A sian vegetables in a light broth make an excellent first course for any day of the week.

Servings: 4~6

6 cups chicken broth

1 teaspoon soy sauce

¼ cup dry sherry

½ cup thinly sliced bok choy

4 oz. enoki mushrooms

4 oz. snow pea pods, sliced

1 egg, beaten

2 green onions, slivered

1 In a large saucepan, combine all ingredients except egg and green onion. Bring soup to a boil.

2 Stirring soup constantly, slowly pour beaten egg into soup Ladle soup into bowls and sprinkle slivered green onions on top. Serve immediately.

Asian Vegetable Soup with Tofu
Add ½ cup cubed tofu in step 1.
Asian Vegetable Soup with Shrimp
Add ½ cup cooked shrimp meat in step 1.

bok choy: also called Chinese white cabbage, bok choy is a type of cabbage common to Chinese cookery. Look for it in a well-stocked supermarket, Asian market or specialty food store.

enoki mushrooms: long, delicate white mushrooms common to Chinese cookery.Look for them in a well-stocked supermarket, Asian market or specialty food store.

Autumn Soup

A touch of nutmeg in this soup is a nice addition. Serve this a first course soup or as a light meal accompanied by fresh bread.

Servings: 4~6

1/4 cup butter

1 yellow onion, chopped

4 cups chopped peeled fresh pumpkin flesh*

2 large potatoes, peeled and chopped

4 carrots, peeled and chopped

4 medium turnips, peeled and chopped

4 cups chicken stock

1/3 cup sherry

1/4 teaspoon ground nutmeg

1/2 teaspoon salt

2 cups half-and-half

*If fresh pumpkin is not available, use 2 cups unseasoned canned pumpkin.

1 In a large soup or stockpot, melt butter over medium heat. Add onion and sauté until translucent.

2 Add remaining vegetables and sauté until onion begins to turn golden. Add chicken stock and bring mixture to a boil. Reduce heat to low, cover and simmer until all vegetables are tender, about 30 minutes (more or less time depending on the size of the chopped vegetables). Cool soup slightly.

3 Puree mixture in 2 or 3 batches in your blender or process with a food processor. Pulse until smooth. Return pureed soup to pot. Add sherry, nutmeg and salt. Bring to a boil over medium-high heat, stirring frequently. Remove from heat. Stir in half-and-half and serve immediately.

Autumn Honey and Pumpkin Soup
Omit turnips from step 2 and add 1/4 cup honey in step 3.

Winter Vegetable Soup
Omit pumpkin and use 4 cups peeled, seeded, chopped banana squash in step 2.

Spring Vegetable Soup
Omit pumpkin and turnips from step 2. After you have pureed soup in step 3, add 3 cups chopped baby crookneck squash and bring mixture to a boil. Simmer only until squash is tender. Add half-and-half and serve.

Butternut Squash Soup

This favorite autumn soup boasts a creamy, smooth texture and a beautiful golden color. If desired, top servings of soup with crunchy homemade croutons.

Servings: 4-6

1 tablespoon butter

1 yellow onion, chopped

1 butternut squash, 2 lb., peeled, seeded and cut into 1-inch cubes

3 cups chicken broth

1/4 teaspoon salt

1/2 cup heavy cream

1 In a medium soup pot, melt butter over medium-high heat.

2 Add chopped onion and cook until translucent.

3 Add squash, chicken broth and salt. Bring mixture to a boil.

4 Reduce heat to low and simmer uncovered for 30 minutes or until squash is soft.

5 Puree soup (in batches if necessary) in a blender container. Blend until smooth and return soup to pot.

6 Bring soup to a boil. Remove from heat and add cream. Stir to mix and serve immediately.

Apple Butternut Squash Soup
In step 4, add 1 large peeled, chopped Granny Smith Apple.

Butternut Squash Soup (low-fat version)
In step 4, add 1 medium peeled, chopped potato. Omit cream in step 6.

Curried Butternut Squash Soup
In step 4, add 1 teaspoon curry powder or to taste.

Golden Mushroom Soup

Browning the mushrooms gives this soup its golden color. A touch of sherry makes it a bit more sophisticated than your canned mushroom soup.

Servings: 4~6

1/2 cup butter

8 cups coarsely chopped fresh white mushrooms

1 large yellow onion, chopped

2 cups chicken broth

1/2 cup dry sherry

1/2 teaspoon salt

1 cup light cream or half-and-half

1 In a large soup pot, melt butter over medium-high heat. When melted, add mushrooms and onion. Sauté over medium-high heat, stirring very frequently. Cook until mushrooms juices are released and mushrooms turn a golden brown.

2 Add chicken broth, sherry and salt. Bring to a boil over medium-high heat, stirring frequently. Reduce heat to low and simmer uncovered for 15 minutes.

3 Remove from heat, add cream and serve immediately.

Mixed Mushroom Soup
Reduce white mushrooms to 4 cups in step 1. Add 1 cup chopped shiitake mushrooms, 1 cup chopped oyster mushrooms, 1 cup chopped portobello mushrooms and 1/2 oz. dried porcini mushrooms (soak porcini mushrooms in 1/2 cup boiling water for 20 minutes to soften). In step 2 omit sherry and use 1/2 cup white wine. Simmer for 20 minutes in step 2.

Golden Mushroom and Potato Soup
Add 2 peeled, chopped Yukon Gold potatoes in step 1. Increase chicken broth to 3 cups in step 2 and simmer for 20 minutes. Increase cream to 1 1/2 cups in step 3.

Cream of Artichoke Soup

Every year in Watsonville, California, there is an artichoke festival where you can try everything from French-fried artichoke hearts to artichoke ice cream. You can also find artichoke soup in many forms. Here is just one of many creations.

Servings: 4~6

2 teaspoons butter

1 yellow onion, chopped

4 cups drained canned artichoke hearts (do not use marinated)

1 large russet potato, peeled and chopped

3 cups chicken broth

1 teaspoon salt

1 cup half-and-half

1 In a large soup pot, melt butter over medium heat. Add onion and sauté until onion is translucent.

2 Add artichoke hearts, potato, chicken broth and salt. Bring mixture to a boil, reduce heat to low and simmer for 15 minutes, or until potatoes and artichoke hearts are tender. Remove from heat and cool slightly.

3 Pour mixture (in batches if necessary) into a blender container. Pulse until smooth. Return soup to soup pot.

4 Bring soup to a boil. Remove from heat and stir in half and-half. Serve immediately.

Cream of Broccoli Soup
Omit artichoke hearts and use 4 cups chopped broccoli in step 2.

Cream of Asparagus Soup
Omit artichoke hearts, and use 4 cups chopped fresh asparagus in step 2.

Cream of Carrot Soup
Omit artichoke hearts and use 4 cups chopped fresh carrots in step 2.

Fiery Cream of Red Pepper Soup

When fresh red bell peppers are in season and inexpensive, take advantage and stock up. Seed them, cut them into quarters and freeze them in plastic bags and you can enjoy this soup anytime of year.

Servings: 4

2 tablespoons butter

1 yellow onion, chopped

3 large red bell peppers, seeded

2 cups chicken broth

1/2 teaspoon ground cumin

1/2 teaspoon salt

1/4 teaspoon cayenne pepper

1/2 cup heavy cream

1 In a large soup pot, melt butter over medium-high heat. Add chopped onion and sauté until translucent, about 5 minutes.

2 Cut red peppers into 1-inch chunks. Add peppers and chicken broth to onions. Bring mixture to a boil. Reduce heat and simmer until peppers are soft, about 15 minutes. Remove from heat.

3 Pour red pepper mixture into a blender container or process with a food processor. Puree soup until smooth and return to soup pot.

4 Add cumin, salt and cayenne pepper. Bring soup to a boil, reduce heat to low and simmer for 5 minutes, stirring frequently.

5 Remove from heat. Pour cream into soup, stirring well. Serve immediately.

Fiery Cream of Yellow Pepper Soup
Substitute yellow bell peppers for red peppers in step 2.

Cream of Roasted Red Pepper Soup
Before cutting peppers, place under a broiler to char skin. Remove peppers from oven and place in a paper bag. Let peppers stand for 5 minutes. Remove any loosened blackened skin and continue with recipe from step 2.

Soups

Roasted Corn Chowder

Roasting the corn for this chowder adds a smoky flavor to the soup, or use frozen corn ears.

Servings: 6~8

4 ears fresh corn, husks and silk removed

8 cups water

1 large potato, peeled and chopped

2 small red-skinned potatoes, chopped

1 yellow onion, chopped

1 cup chopped celery

1½ teaspoons salt

1 cup milk

1 Prepare medium hot coals in a outdoor barbecue. Place corn on the grill and cook until corn just begins to brown, turning frequently. Corn should be evenly roasted on all sides. Remove from grill and cool.

2 Remove corn from cobs, reserving cobs.

3 In a large stockpot, combine corn cobs, water and peeled potato. Bring to a boil over high heat, reduce heat to low, cover and simmer for 30 minutes.

4 Remove cobs from water. Place cooked potato and 2 cups of the corn stock in a blender container. Blend on high until smooth. Return potato puree to the stockpot.

5 Add shucked corn, red potatoes, onion, celery and salt to corn stock. Bring soup to a boil; reduce heat to low. Simmer uncovered for 20 minutes or until potatoes are tender and soup is thickened.

6 Remove from heat. Add milk and serve immediately.

Fresh Corn Chowder

Omit step 1. Begin preparing from step 2 and continue on through step 6.

Smoky Roasted Corn Chowder

Add 1 cup chopped, cooked smoked sausage or ham in step 5.

Spring Vegetable and Roasted Corn Chowder

Add 1 1/2 cups coarsely chopped summer squash and 1 cup chopped carrots in step 5.

Roasted Corn and Red Pepper Chowder

Add 1/2 cup chopped, roasted red bell peppers in step 6.

Black Bean Soup with Sausage

The sausage's smoky flavor helps create a very complex set of flavors in this soup. It is wonderful served with your favorite cornbread.

Servings: 6~8

6 slices bacon

1 yellow onion, chopped

3 cans (15 oz. each) black beans, rinsed and drained

2 cans (14½ oz. each) chicken broth

1½ cups sliced or crumbled cooked smoked sausage

1 cup corn kernels

1 cup chopped carrots

1 cup chopped celery

½ teaspoon freshly ground black pepper

1 In a large soup pot, cook bacon over medium-high heat until crisp. Remove bacon and drain all but 1 tablespoon fat from pot. Crumble bacon and set aside.

2 Return pot to heat and add onion. Sauté until translucent, stirring frequently.

3 Place 2 cans drained beans and 1 can chicken broth in a blender container or food processor workbowl. Pulse until smooth. Add to cooked onions in soup pot.

4 Add remaining can beans and remaining can broth to pot. Add bacon, sausage, corn, carrots, celery and pepper. Bring soup to a boil.

5 Reduce heat to low and cover. Simmer for 30 minutes and serve hot.

Black Bean Soup with Ham
Omit sausage from step 4 and add 1½ cups chopped ham.

Arizona Black Bean Soup
In step 4, add 1 chipotle pepper (seeded and chopped), 3/4 teaspoon cumin and 1 cup chopped red bell pepper.

Italian Meatball Soup

Some Italian restaurants call this "Italian Wedding Soup." It is a very filling soup and can be added to your favorite type of pasta and vegetables. Fresh sourdough bread completes the meal.

Servings: 6~8

¾ lb. ground beef

¼ lb. Italian sausage

½ cup dry breadcrumbs

2 eggs

1 yellow onion, chopped

8 cups beef broth

½ teaspoon dried oregano

2 cups chopped peeled tomatoes

2 carrots, peeled and chopped

2 stalks celery, chopped

2 cups chopped fresh Swiss chard or kale

1 In a medium bowl, combine ground beef, Italian sausage, breadcrumbs and eggs. Mix well and shape into 1-inch meatballs.

2 Heat a large soup pot over medium heat. Add meatballs and cook until lightly browned. Remove meatballs and set aside; drain excess fat from pot.

3 Return pot to stove over medium heat, add onion and sauté until translucent. Add remaining ingredients and increase heat to high. Bring mixture to a boil; reduce heat to low. Add cooked meatballs and simmer for 20 minutes or until carrots are tender. Serve hot.

Italian Meatball and Tortellini Soup
Add ¼ lb. cooked tortellini at the end of step 3, just before serving.

Italian Tortellini Soup
Omit meatballs (ground beef, Italian sausage, breadcrumbs and eggs) in steps 1 and 2.

Shrimp Bisque

Bisques usually contain seafood and cream and are thickened with rice or breadcrumbs. This version uses tomatoes for a creamy red color.

Servings: 6~8

1/4 cup butter

2 stalks celery, chopped

1/2 yellow onion, chopped

1/2 cup dry white wine

6 cups chicken or vegetable broth

1/2 cup uncooked white rice

2 cups peeled chopped fresh tomatoes

1 teaspoon salt

1/4 teaspoon cayenne pepper

1 lb. medium shrimp, cooked and peeled

1 cup heavy cream

1 In a large soup pot, melt butter over medium heat. Add celery and onion and sauté until vegetables are tender.

2 Add wine, broth, rice, tomatoes, salt and cayenne pepper. Bring soup to a boil, cover and reduce heat to low. Simmer for 20 minutes, or until rice is tender

3 Puree soup (in batches if necessary) in a blender container until smooth. Return to soup pot.

4 Bring soup to a boil. Add shrimp meat and heavy cream. Stir to mix and serve immediately (do not let soup boil once cream has been added).

Crab Bisque
Omit shrimp meat from step 4 and use 1 lb. cooked crabmeat.

Lobster Bisque
Omit shrimp meat from step 4 and use 1 lb. cooked lobster meat.

Seafood Bisque
Reduce shrimp meat to 1/2 cup and add 1/3 cup cooked crabmeat and 1/3 cup cooked lobster meat in step 4.

Side Dishes

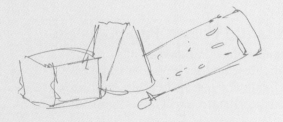

Side Dishes

Broccoli with Sesame Butter 82
Sugar Snap Peas with Sesame Butter
Zucchini with Sesame Butter
Baby Bok Choy with Sesame Butter

Oven-Roasted Tomatoes 83
Oregano Roasted Tomatoes
Basil Roasted Tomatoes
Tarragon Roasted Tomatoes

Ratatouille 84
Chicken Ratatouille
Shrimp Ratatouille

Buttermilk Mashed Potatoes 85
Sour Cream Mashed Potatoes
Sour Cream and Chive Mashed Potaotes
Buttermilk and Bacon Mashed Potatoes

Delicate Potato Pancakes 86
Rustic Potato Pancakes
Delicate Cheddar Potato Pancakes
Delicate Carrot and Potato Pancakes
Delicate Potato and Chive Pancakes

Mustard Roasted Potatoes 87
Rosemary and Mustard Roasted Potatoes
Dijon Roasted Potatoes

Polenta 88
Herbed Polenta
Garlic Polenta
Sun-Dried Tomato Polenta

Artichoke Rice 89
Brown and Wild Artichoke Rice
Artichoke and Pepper Jack Rice

Florentine Rice 90
Florentine Parmesan Rice
Swiss Chard Rice

Vegetable Fried Rice 91
Chicken Fried Rice
Shrimp Fried Rice
Pork Fried Rice

Chorizo Rice 92
Widly Hot and Spicy Chorizo Rice
Sausage Rice
Italian-Style Sausage and Rice

Parmesan Rice Cakes 93
Rice Cakes
Parmesan Brown Rice Cakes
Parmesan Wild Rice Cakes

Baked Parmesan Risotto 94
Baked Romano Risotto
Baked Cheddar Risotto
Baked Parmesan Risotto with Chives

Red Chard Risotto 95
Spinach Risotto
Artichoke Risotto
Asparagus Risotto

Fresh Herb Pasta 96
Fresh Herb and Cream Pasta
Fresh Herb and Parmesan Pasta

Broccoli with Sesame Butter

Vegetables cooked tender-crisp need only the simplest sauce to complement their flavors. Here, sesame butter adds an Asian touch to steamed fresh broccoli.

Servings: 4-6

1 teaspoon sesame seeds

1 lb. broccoli florets

¼ cup butter

4 teaspoons soy sauce

½ teaspoon sesame oil

1 Heat a small skillet over medium heat. Add sesame seeds and sauté until light golden brown; stir constantly to prevent burning. Remove from skillet and set aside.

2 In a steamer or covered saucepan with a steamer insert, steam broccoli until tender-crisp.

3 While broccoli is steaming, melt butter in a small saucepan over medium heat. Add soy sauce and sesame oil and remove from heat.

4 Drain broccoli and place in a serving bowl. Pour butter sauce over broccoli and toss to coat. Sprinkle broccoli with toasted sesame seeds and serve immediately.

Sugar Snap Peas with Sesame Butter
Substitute sugar snap peas for broccoli florets.

Zucchini with Sesame Butter
Substitute sliced zucchini for broccoli florets.

Baby Bok Choy with Sesame Butter
Substitute sliced baby bok choy for broccoli florets.

Oven~Roasted Tomatoes

Roasting tomatoes makes their flavor much more intense. Roma tomatoes are a perfect choice for this recipe because they have a lot of tomato flesh for their size and few seeds.

Servings: 4

4 ripe Roma tomatoes

2 teaspoons olive oil

Preheat oven to 250°.

1 Slice tomatoes in half lengthwise. Place tomatoes, skin side down, on a baking sheet.

2 Drizzle 1/4 teaspoon olive oil over each tomato half.

3 Place pan in oven. Roast for 3 hours and serve immediately.

Oregano Roasted Tomatoes
After drizzling oil in step 2, sprinkle 1/8 teaspoon crumbled, dried oregano over each half (or use 1/4 teaspoon fresh oregano on each half).

Basil Roasted Tomatoes
After drizzling oil in step 2, sprinkle 1/8 teaspoon crumbled, dried basil over each half (or use 1/4 teaspoon fresh basil on each half).

Tarragon Roasted Tomatoes
After drizzling oil in step 2, sprinkle 1/8 teaspoon crumbled, dried tarragon over each half (or use 1/4 teaspoon fresh tarragon on each half).

Ratatouille

Ratatouille is delicious hot and cold. Varying the vegetables to your personal style and choosing seasonal vegetables will complement this dish.

Servings: 6~8

1 eggplant

½ teaspoon salt

2 tablespoons olive oil

2 cloves garlic, chopped

1 yellow onion, chopped

1 green bell pepper, seeded and chopped

2 stalks celery, sliced

4 cups peeled tomatoes with juice

¼ cup chopped fresh Italian parsley

¼ teaspoon dried thyme

2 bay leaves

½ cup red wine

1 Peel eggplant and cut into 1-inch cubes. Place eggplant in a colander and sprinkle with salt. Set aside for 20 minutes.

2 Heat olive oil in a large pot over medium-high heat. Add garlic and onion and sauté until onion and garlic begin to brown.

3 Add eggplant and all other ingredients. Bring to a boil, reduce heat to low, cover and simmer for 20 minutes. Serve hot or place in refrigerator and serve cold.

Chicken Ratatouille
Add 2 cups chopped or sliced cooked chicken in step 3, about 5 minutes before serving.

Shrimp Ratatouille
Add 2 cups cooked shrimp meat in step 3, about 5 minutes before serving.

Buttermilk Mashed Potatoes

The extra texture from these potatoes will remind you of the "hominess" of the holidays. Using a hand masher helps keep these potatoes from becoming too smooth.

Servings: 6~8

2½ lb. red-skinned potatoes

2 tablespoons butter

1 cup buttermilk

¾ teaspoon salt

½ teaspoon pepper

1 Cut potatoes into large chunks (do not peel). Place potatoes in a large pot and add water to cover. Place pot on high heat and bring potatoes to a boil. Reduce heat to medium and cook until potatoes are tender.

2 Remove from heat and drain potatoes. In a large bowl, mash potatoes with a masher or a pastry cutter (potatoes should not be smooth, do not use a mixer.) Add butter and stir until butter is melted. Stir in buttermilk, salt and pepper and mix well. Serve immediately.

Sour Cream Mashed Potatoes
Use 1 cup sour cream in place of buttermilk in step 2.

Sour Cream and Chive Mashed Potatoes
Use 1 cup sour cream in place of buttermilk in step 2. Add ½ cup minced chives in step 2 when you add sour cream.

Buttermilk and Bacon Mashed Potatoes
Add ½ cup cooked crumbled bacon in step 2 when you add buttermilk.

Delicate Potato Pancakes

Place the shredded potatoes in water to wash away some of the potato starch. This helps the potato pancakes stay light in texture.

Servings: 6~8

3 medium-sized baking potatoes, peeled

2 tablespoons minced yellow onion

2 eggs, beaten

2 tablespoons all-purpose flour

1 teaspoon salt

¼ teaspoon baking powder

vegetable shortening for frying

1 Fill a large bowl halfway with cold water. Shred potatoes into water and let stand while preparing batter.

2 In a large bowl, mix together onion, eggs, flour, salt and baking powder, stirring to mix well.

3 Drain potatoes in a colander, shaking to remove excess water. Add potatoes to flour mixture and stir to mix.

4 Heat a large nonstick skillet or griddle over medium-high heat. Add 1 tablespoon shortening. Pour batter in 1/3 cups into skillet and cook for 10 minutes per side or until deep golden brown, turning only once. Serve hot.

Rustic Potato Pancakes
Omit 3 peeled potatoes and use 3 unpeeled potatoes in step 1.

Delicate Cheddar Potato Pancakes
Add 1/2 cup shredded extra-sharp cheddar cheese in step 3 when you add potatoes in step 3.

Delicate Carrot and Potato Pancakes
Add 1/2 cup shredded carrots in step 3 when you add potatoes.

Delicate Potato and Chive Pancakes
Add 2 tablespoons minced chives in step 2 when you add potatoes.

Mustard Roasted Potatoes

Oven-roasted potatoes are a classic side dish. With the addition of mustard and herbs, you have a side dish that can stand up to any pork, beef or chicken entrée.

Servings: 6-8

1½ lb. red-skinned potatoes

1 yellow onion, chopped

2 tablespoons olive oil

2 tablespoons grainy mustard

½ teaspoon salt

½ teaspoon freshly ground black pepper

Preheat oven to 400°. Prepare a 9-x-9-inch baking dish by spraying with nonstick cooking spray.

1 Scrub potatoes and cut into large chunks. Place potatoes in a large bowl.

2 Add onion, olive oil, mustard, salt and pepper to potatoes. Toss to coat well.

3 Turn mixture into prepared baking dish and place in oven. Roast until potatoes are tender, about 45 to 60 minutes, depending on size of chunks. Serve hot.

Rosemary and Mustard Roasted Potatoes
Add 1 tablespoon chopped fresh rosemary in step 2.

Dijon Roasted Potatoes
Omit coarse grained mustard in step 2 and use 2 tablespoons Dijon mustard.

Polenta

Polenta is served as a side dish in Italy, similar to serving rice or potatoes in this country. You can add many ingredients to a basic polenta recipe, such as cooked, chopped meats, chunks of cheese or cooked vegetables, to create a signature entrée.

Servings: 6~8

4 cups chicken broth or water

2 tablespoons butter

1 cup polenta

½ teaspoon salt

Preheat oven to 350°.

1 In a medium saucepan over high heat, bring chicken broth or water and butter to a boil.

2 Remove from heat and stir in polenta and salt. Turn polenta into a 2-quart covered casserole dish, cover and place in oven.

3 Bake for 25 minutes. Remove from oven, stir and serve immediately.

Herbed Polenta
Add ¾ teaspoon dried basil and ¾ teaspoon dried oregano in step 2.

Garlic Polenta
In a small skillet, melt 1 tablespoon butter over medium heat. Add 6 cloves garlic, minced. Sauté until garlic just begins to brown, about 3 minutes. Add garlic and butter to polenta in step 2.

Sun-Dried Tomato Polenta
Add 2 tablespoons minced sun-dried tomatoes in step 2.

Artichoke Rice

Subtly flavored, this rice can accompany some of your favorite bold-flavored main dishes. The wild rice variation adds a touch of elegance to your meal.

Servings: 4~6

2 tablespoons
vegetable oil

1 cup
long-grain rice

1 yellow onion,
minced

2 cups water or
vegetable broth

1⅓ cups chopped
artichoke hearts

1 teaspoon salt

½ teaspoon freshly
ground black pepper

1 In a large saucepan, heat oil over medium high heat. Add rice and sauté until rice turns translucent.

2 Add onion and continue to sauté until rice is begins to brown and onions are translucent, about 5 minutes.

3 Add water or broth, artichoke hearts, salt and pepper. Bring mixture to a boil, reduce heat to low, cover and simmer until rice is tender, about 15 minutes. Serve immediately.

Brown and Wild Artichoke Rice
Omit long-grain rice. Use ½ cup brown rice and ½ cup wild rice in step 1. Increase water to 1¼ cups.

Artichoke and Pepper Jack Rice
Add 1 cup shredded pepper Jack cheese after rice has cooked at end of step 3. Add cheese and stir to mix. Stir until cheese has melted and is evenly distributed. Serve immediately.

Florentine Rice

This side dish is very colorful. It makes a nice change from plain rice or potatoes on your dinner plate.

Servings: 4-6

1 tablespoon butter

1 yellow onion, minced

1 cup long-grain rice

2½ cups chicken broth

1 pkg. (10 oz.) frozen chopped spinach, thawed

¼ teaspoon freshly ground nutmeg

½ teaspoon salt

1 In a medium saucepan, melt butter over medium-high heat. Add onion and sauté until translucent.

2 Add rice and 2 cups of the chicken broth to saucepan. Increase heat to high and bring mixture to a boil, stirring occasionally. Reduce heat to low, cover and simmer for 15 minutes.

3 Squeeze spinach until dry. Add remaining ½ cup broth, spinach, nutmeg and salt to rice. Stir to mix, cover and return to low heat. Continue to cook for another 5 to 8 minutes or until rice is tender, but not soft. Serve immediately.

Florentine Parmesan Rice
Add 1 cup shredded Parmesan cheese just prior to serving, mixing it well into the rice.

Swiss Chard Rice
Use 1 cup cooked Swiss chard (red or green chard) instead of spinach in step 3.

Vegetable Fried Rice

This side dish can be a full meal when teamed with a light soup. Fried rice is best when you use rice that was cooked the day before you make it.

Servings: 6~8

2 tablespoons vegetable oil

2 eggs

1 yellow onion, chopped

2 carrots, peeled and chopped

3 stalks celery, chopped

1 cup chopped fresh white mushrooms

4 cups cooked white rice

1 tablespoon soy sauce

1 cup sliced snow pea pods

1 In a wok or a large skillet, heat 1 teaspoon of the oil over medium heat. Beat eggs and pour into wok. Scramble eggs until done, and remove from wok; set aside.

2 Heat 2 teaspoons oil in wok. Add onion, carrots, celery and mushrooms. Stir-fry on high heat until mushroom liquid is released and liquid has evaporated. Vegetables should be tender-crisp. Remove vegetables from wok and set aside.

3 Heat remaining 1 tablespoon oil in wok on high heat. Add rice and stir-fry rice until hot. Add soy sauce and toss to mix well.

4 Add cooked egg, cooked vegetables and pea pods or peas to rice. Stir fry on high heat until pea pods are tender-crisp. Serve immediately.

Chicken Fried Rice
Add 1 cup chopped, cooked chicken in step 4. Stir-fry until all ingredients are hot.

Shrimp Fried Rice
Add 1 cup cooked shrimp meat in step 4. Stir-fry until all ingredients are heated through.

Pork Fried Rice
Add 1 cup cooked pork in step 4. Stir-fry until all ingredients are heated through.

Chorizo Rice

A variation of Spanish rice uses spicy Mexican chorizo sausage as a main element. Chorizo is available in bulk or in links. If using links, remove the sausage from casings before proceeding.

Servings: 4~6

3/4 lb. mild chorizo sausage

1/2 green bell pepper, seeded and chopped

3 cups chopped tomatoes

1/2 teaspoon ground cumin

1/2 teaspoon salt

1 cup long-grain white rice

1 In a medium saucepan, crumble chorizo. Cook over medium-high heat until lightly browned. Drain all excess fat.

2 Add all remaining ingredients and stir to mix. Increase heat to high. Bring mixture to a boil, reduce heat to low, cover and simmer until rice is tender, about 20 minutes. Serve immediately.

Wildly Hot and Spicy Chorizo Rice
Omit mild chorizo and use 1/2 lb. hot chorizo in step 1. Add 1 can (4 oz.) chopped jalapeño peppers in step 2.

Sausage Rice
Omit chorizo in step 1 and use 1/2 lb. pork sausage.

Italian-Style Sausage and Rice
Omit chorizo in step 1 and use 1/2 lb. Italian sausage. Omit cumin and add 1/2 teaspoon dried oregano or dried basil in step 2.

Parmesan Rice Cakes

These are an interesting departure from plain rice. They can be assembled early in the day and sautéed right before serving time.

Servings: 6~8

2 cups cooked
white rice

1/2 cup chopped
fresh chives

1 cup fresh
breadcrumbs

3 eggs

1/2 cup freshly grated
Parmesan cheese

3/4 teaspoon salt

vegetable oil
for frying

1 Combine all ingredients. Form into 1/4 cup patties, pressing firmly.

2 Heat a large skillet over medium heat. Pour 1 teaspoon oil into skillet. Place a few patties in skillet, making sure not to overcrowd. Fry until cakes are golden brown on both sides, about 5 minutes per side. Keep warm while cooking remaining cakes. Serve immediately.

Rice Cakes
Omit Parmesan cheese.

Parmesan Brown Rice Cakes
Use 2 cups cooked brown rice instead of white rice in step 1.

Parmesan Wild Rice Cakes
Use 1 cup cooked wild rice with 1 cup cooked white rice in step 1.

Baked Parmesan Risotto

Though not a true risotto, this still uses the typical short-grained Arborio rice. You can make it a bit more true-to-form by stirring in ½ cup of hot chicken broth just before serving.

Servings: 4~6

2 tablespoons butter

1 cup Arborio rice

½ cup dry white wine

2 cups chicken broth

½ teaspoon salt

½ cup freshly grated Parmesan cheese

Preheat oven to 400°. Prepare a large covered casserole dish by spraying sides and bottom with nonstick spray.

1 In a medium saucepan over medium-high heat, melt butter.

2 Add rice and stir constantly. Cook until rice begins to turn translucent, about 2 minutes.

3 Add white wine and stir constantly until wine is absorbed.

4 Add broth and salt and bring to a boil.

5 Remove from heat and stir in Parmesan. Transfer rice mixture to prepared casserole. Cover and bake for 35 minutes (rice should still be a bit firm). Serve immediately.

Baked Romano Risotto
Substitute Romano cheese for Parmesan in step 5.

Baked Cheddar Risotto
Substitute sharp cheddar cheese for Parmesan in step 5.

Baked Parmesan Risotto with Chives
Add ¼ cup minced chives when you add Parmesan cheese in step 5.

Red Chard Risotto

This risotto is full of flavorful Swiss chard and turns it a light pink color. Regular green chard works just as well and will make a pretty green-flecked side dish.

Servings: 6-8

5 cups chicken broth

2 tablespoons olive oil

1 medium-sized yellow onion, minced

1½ cups Arborio rice

4 cups fresh red Swiss chard leaves, coarsely chopped

½ cup dry white wine

½ cup freshly grated Parmesan cheese

salt to taste

1 Heat broth to just boiling in a saucepan. Lower heat and maintain a gentle simmer.

2 Heat olive oil in a large saucepan over medium heat. Add onion and sauté for 2 to 3 minutes, until clear but not browned. Add rice and Swiss chard and stir for 1 minute to thoroughly coat rice and chard with oil.

3 Add wine and stir constantly until wine is absorbed. Add stock ½ cup at a time, stirring thoroughly after each addition. Continue to add broth as it is absorbed (about 2 to 3 minutes), ½ cup at a time. It will take about 20 minutes to cook (it is best to have rice tender, but *al dente*). Use all broth.

4 Remove risotto from heat, stir in Parmesan and add salt to taste if needed. Serve immediately.

Spinach Risotto
Omit Swiss chard and use 4 cups chopped fresh spinach in step 2.

Artichoke Risotto
Omit Swiss chard and use 2 cups chopped artichoke hearts in step 2.

Asparagus Risotto
Omit Swiss chard and add 2 cups sliced asparagus when you add the last of the broth. Cook risotto until asparagus is tender-crisp; continue with step 4

Side Dishes

95

Fresh Herb Pasta

This recipe is one of the best reasons to grow a miniature herb garden. Snip some fresh herbs as the pasta cooks and toss them into the finished dish. There is no easier or fresher way to present pasta.

Servings: 4~6

12 oz. dried
angel hair pasta

⅓ cup butter

2 tablespoons
olive oil

2 cloves garlic,
minced

¼ cup chopped
fresh chives

⅓ cup chopped
fresh Italian parsley

½ cup chopped
fresh basil

1 Begin cooking pasta according to package directions. While pasta is cooking, begin making sauce.

2 In a small saucepan, melt butter over medium heat. When melted, add olive oil and garlic. Continue to cook over medium heat until garlic just begins to brown. Remove from heat.

3 When pasta is done, drain. Place pasta in a large serving bowl. Pour garlic butter mixture over pasta and toss to coat. Add chives, parsley and basil. Toss to mix thoroughly and serve immediately.

Fresh Herb and Cream Pasta

Omit butter and use cream in step 1. Cook garlic in olive oil in step 2. Remove from heat and add 1/2 cup heavy cream.

Fresh Herb and Parmesan Pasta

Add 1/2 cup freshly grated Parmesan cheese in step 3.

Entrées

Entrées

Pasta Puttanesca 104
Chicken Pasta Puttanesca
Shrimp Pasta Puttanesca
Clam Pasta Puttanesca

Baked Three-Cheese Rigatoni 105
Baked Cheese Rigatoni with Sausage
Baked Cheese Rigatoni with Tomatoes

Fettucine with Tomato-Mushroom Sauce 106
Fettucine with Tomato-Mushroom and Red Wine Sauce
Fettucine with Tomato-Mushroom Cream Sauce
Tomato-Mushroom Lasagna

Fettucine with Scallops and Garlic Cream Sauce 108
Fettucine with Garlic Cream Sauce
Fettucine with Shrimp and Garlic Cream Sauce

Seafood Jambalaya 110
Seafood and Chicken Jambalaya
Seafood and Pork Jambalaya
Seafood and Sausage Jambalaya

Creole Snapper 111
Creole Sole
Creole Turbot

Trout with Balsamic Sauce 112
Trout with Balsamic Basil Sauce
Trout with Balsamic Lemon Sauce

Grilled Tuna with Cilantro-Lime Butter 113
Grilled Tuna with Parsley-Lemon Butter
Grilled Tuna with Caper-Lemon Butter

Caribbean Chicken 114
Caribbean Spareribs
Caribbean Pork Chops

Chicken and Mushrooms with Mustard-Brandy Sauce 115

Chicken with Mustard-Brandy Sauce
Chicken with Mustard-Sherry Sauce
Chicken and Mushrooms with Brandy
 Sauce

Stir-Fried Chicken with Two Onions 116

Stir-Fried Beef with Two Onions
Stir-Fried Chicken with Wine and
 Two Onions
Stir-Fried Chicken with Yellow Onions

Grilled Chicken Breasts with Outback Salsa 117

Grilled Chicken Breasts with Volcano
 Salsa
Grilled Chicken Breasts with Carribean
 Salsa

Braised Chicken with Artichokes and Tomatoes 118

Braised Chicken Breasts with Artichokes
 and Tomatoes
Braised Chicken with White Wine and
 Artichokes

Roasted Chicken with Fresh Sage 119

Roasted Chicken with Fresh Sage and
 Lemon
Roasted Chicken with Fresh Thyme
Roasted Chicken with Fresh Chervil

Roasted Chicken with Rice-Walnut Stuffing 120

Roasted Chicken with Rice-Hazelnut
 Stuffing
Roasted Chicken with Rice-Cashew
 Stuffing

Chipotle Pork Stew 122

Chipotle Pork and Vegetable Stew
Saucy Chipotle Pork Ribs

Honey-Mustard Pork Tenderloin 123

Maple-Mustard Pork Tenderloin
Orange-Mustard Pork Tenderloin

Pork Chops with Orange-Boubon Sauce 124

Pork Chops with Orange Sauce
Pork Chops and Apples with Orange-Bourbon Sauce

Italian Beef Stew 125

Italian Beef Stew with Vegetables
Herbed Italian Beef Stew

Beef Roast with Winter Vegetables 126

Beef Roast with Spring Vegetables
Beef Roast with Autumn Vegetables

Garlic Beef Provençal with Leeks 128

Garlic Beef Provençal
Garlic Beef Provençal with Onions
Beef Provençal

Mexican Flank Steak 130

Mexican Flank Steak with Peppers
Mexican Flank Steak with Smoky Onions

Pan-Seared Filet Mignon with Brie Sauce 131

Pan-Seared Filet Mignon with Herbed Brie Sauce
Pan-Seared Filet Mignon with Peppercorn Brie Sauce
Pan-Seared Filet Mignon with Gorgonzola Sauce

Grilled Filet Mignon with Chile Butter 132

Grilled Filet Mignon with Blue Cheese Butter
Grilled Filet Mignon with Garlic Herb Butter

Pasta Puttanesca

This pasta sauce is fast and easy to prepare and it's full of summer flavors. You can use either peeled fresh tomatoes or canned tomatoes, depending on what you have on hand.

Servings: 4-6

2 tablespoons olive oil

2 cloves garlic, minced

1 yellow onion, chopped

2 tablespoons capers, rinsed

4 cups chopped peeled fresh tomatoes

1/2 teaspoon dried oregano

1/2 teaspoon dried basil

1/2 teaspoon salt

1 lb. linguini

1. In a large pot, heat oil over medium-high heat. Add garlic and onion and sauté for about 5 minutes, until onion begins to brown.

2. Add capers, tomatoes, oregano, basil and salt and bring mixture to a boil. Reduce heat to medium-low and simmer uncovered for 20 minutes, stirring frequently.

3. Cook pasta in a large pot of boiling salted water according to package directions. Drain pasta and place in a serving bowl. Pour hot sauce over pasta and toss until well mixed. Serve immediately.

Chicken Pasta Puttanesca
Add 2 cups chopped cooked chicken in step 2, about 5 minutes before serving.

Shrimp Pasta Puttanesca
Add 1 1/2 cups cooked peeled shrimp in step 2, about 5 minutes before serving.

Clam Pasta Puttanesca
Add 1 cup chopped cooked clams with their juice in step 2, about 5 minutes before serving.

Baked Three-Cheese Rigatoni

Y ou'll love this very rich, upscale version of macaroni and cheese. It can be made ahead of time through step 3, refrigerated, finished in the oven and served later.

Servings: 4~6

1 lb. rigatoni

¼ cup butter

¼ cup flour

4 cups milk

1½ teaspoons salt

¼ teaspoon ground nutmeg

1½ cups shredded mozzarella cheese

1 pkg. (15 oz.) ricotta cheese

½ cup freshly grated Parmesan cheese

*Use ziti, penne or any other tubular pasta instead of rigatoni.

Preheat oven to 350°. Spray a 9-x-13-inch baking dish with nonstick cooking spray.

1 Cook rigatoni in a large pot of boiling salted water according to package directions; drain and keep warm.

2 While pasta is cooking, melt butter over medium heat in a large saucepan. Add flour and stir with a wire whisk until smooth. Cook, stirring constantly, until mixture bubbles. Add a small amount of milk and stir until smooth. Stir in remaining milk and cook, stirring constantly, until mixture boils. Reduce heat to low and cook for 10 minutes, stirring frequently. Remove mixture from heat.

3 Add salt, nutmeg, 1 cup of the mozzarella cheese, ricotta cheese and Parmesan. Stir until cheeses are melted.

4 Add cooked rigatoni to cheese sauce and stir until very well mixed. Pour pasta and cheese mixture into baking dish and sprinkle with remaining ½ cup mozzarella. Bake for 45 minutes, until browned on top and bubbly.

Baked Cheese Rigatoni with Sausage
Mix 1 cup chopped or thinly sliced cooked smoked sausage or Italian sausage with pasta in step 4.

Baked Cheese Rigatoni with Tomatoes
Mix 1 cup chopped fresh tomatoes with pasta in step 4.

Entrées

Fettuccine with Tomato~Mushroom Sauce

Although porcini mushrooms are expensive, they add a depth of flavor to this sauce that no other mushroom can replace. Substitute your favorite shape of pasta for the fettuccine.

Servings: 4~6

½ oz. dried porcini mushrooms

½ cup boiling water

1 lb. fettuccine

¼ cup olive oil

1 yellow onion, chopped

2 cups chopped white mushrooms

1½ cups chopped shiitake mushrooms

2 cloves garlic, minced

1 can (28 oz.) crushed red tomatoes

1 In a small bowl, combine porcini mushrooms and boiling water and let stand for 20 minutes. Drain mushrooms, reserving liquid. Chop mushrooms and set aside.

2 Cook fettuccine in a large pot of boiling salted water according to package directions; drain and keep warm.

3 In a large pot, heat oil over medium-high heat. Add onion and sauté until beginning to brown. Add white mushrooms, shiitake mushrooms and garlic. Reduce heat to medium and sauté for about 5 minutes, until mushrooms are tender.

4 Add chopped porcini mushrooms, mushroom liquid and tomatoes. Simmer uncovered for 10 minutes.

5 Transfer fettuccine to a warm serving bowl and pour hot sauce over the top. Toss until mixed and serve immediately.

Fettuccine with Tomato-Mushroom and Red Wine Sauce

Add 1/2 cup red wine in step 4.

Fettuccine with Tomato-Mushroom Cream Sauce

After sauce has simmered for 10 minutes in step 4, remove from heat and stir in 1/2 cup heavy cream. Proceed with recipe.

Tomato-Mushroom Lasagna

In step 2, add lasagna sheets to water, proceed with recipe and layer sauce over lasagna sheets. Bake until hot and bubbly.

Fettuccine with Scallops and Garlic Cream Sauce

Pulsing the sauce in a food processor helps to lighten its texture. Take care not to overprocess or you will wind up with whipped cream.

Servings: 4

2 bulbs garlic

4 tablespoons olive oil

2 tablespoons butter

1 lb. sea scallops

2 cups heavy cream

1 teaspoon salt

1 lb. fettuccine

½ cup shredded Parmesan cheese

Preheat oven to 325°.

1. Lay two sheets of aluminum foil on top of each other on a work surface. Place garlic on foil. Pour olive oil over garlic and tightly seal foil around garlic. Bake for about 1 hour and 15 minutes. Remove from oven and cool in foil.

2. In a large skillet, melt butter over medium-low heat. Add scallops and sauté until scallops are just tender, about 10 to 15 minutes.

3. Squeeze soft garlic pulp from papery skin into a blender container or food processor workbowl; discard skin.

4. Add cream and salt to blender container and pulse until smooth. Pour cream mixture into a small saucepan and heat over low heat until very warm. Take care that mixture does not boil.

5. Cook pasta in a large pot of boiling salted water according to package directions; drain. Transfer pasta to a large warm serving bowl.

6. Pour cream sauce over pasta and toss to coat evenly. Sprinkle Parmesan cheese over pasta. Arrange scallops on top of pasta and serve immediately.

Fettuccine with Garlic Cream Sauce

Omit butter and scallops from step 2.

Fettuccine with Shrimp and Garlic Cream Sauce

Substitute shelled raw shrimp for scallops in step 2. Cook shrimp for about 8 minutes or until pink.

Seafood Jambalaya

To customize this basic Creole-style stew, add sausage, ham, pork ribs, cooked bacon or any other item on hand.

Servings: 6~8

2 tablespoons vegetable oil

1 yellow onion, chopped

1 cup chopped celery

1 cup chopped green bell pepper

2 cloves garlic, minced

1 cup long-grain rice

1 teaspoon salt

½ teaspoon crushed red pepper flakes

1 teaspoon dried thyme

2 cups vegetable broth

2 bay leaves

1 pint clams

1 lb. shelled raw shrimp

1 crab, cleaned and cracked

1 can (16 oz.) tomatoes

1 In a large soup pot, heat oil over medium heat. Add onion, celery, bell pepper and garlic and sauté until onion is translucent and celery and bell pepper are bright green.

2 Add rice, salt, pepper flakes and thyme and stir to coat rice with oil. Add broth and bay leaves and bring mixture to a boil. Reduce heat to low, cover and simmer for about 15 minutes, until rice is barely tender.

3 Stir in clams, shrimp, crab and tomatoes. Cover and simmer for 10 minutes. Remove bay leaves and serve immediately.

Seafood and Chicken Jambalaya
Add 2 cups cubed cooked chicken meat with seafood in step 3.

Seafood and Pork Jambalaya
Add 1 lb. baby back pork ribs in step 1. Sauté until ribs are lightly browned. (Have your butcher cut ribs into 2-inch pieces.)

Seafood and Sausage Jambalaya
Add 1 lb. cubed cooked smoked sausage with seafood in step 3.

Creole Snapper

Old Bay Seasoning is most commonly used for boiling shrimp and crab. It also makes a wonderful all-purpose seasoning for both seafood and chicken. You can spice up this recipe by adding a pinch (or several pinches) of dried red chiles to the seasoning mixture.

Servings: 4

1 teaspoon
Old Bay Seasoning

1 clove garlic, minced

¼ teaspoon salt

3 tablespoons
butter, melted

4 red snapper fillets,
about 6 oz. each

Preheat broiler.

1 In a small bowl, combine Old Bay Seasoning, garlic, salt and butter. Stir until well mixed.

2 Place snapper fillets on a broiler pan. Brush the tops of fish with ½ of the butter mixture. Broil for 3 minutes.

3 Baste with remaining butter mixture and broil for 3 to 5 minutes, or until fish is cooked through and flakes easily with a fork. Serve immediately.

Creole Sole
Substitute sole fillets for snapper fillets in step 2.

Creole Turbot
Substitute turbot fillets for snapper fillets in step 2.

Entrées

Trout with Balsamic Sauce

Mild-tasting balsamic vinegar makes a nice sauce for an easy-to-prepare fish dish. Tailor the sauce to your personal taste by adding fresh herbs.

Servings: 4

3 tablespoons
olive oil

4 medium trout fillets

½ cup butter

1 tablespoon flour

¼ cup
balsamic vinegar

2 tablespoons
sliced green onions

1 Heat olive oil over medium-high heat in a sauté pan and sauté fillets for 2 minutes on each side, or until golden brown.

2 In a small saucepan, melt butter over low heat. Add flour and stir until well blended. Cook mixture, stirring, for 4 minutes, taking care that it does not scorch.

3 Remove from heat. Add balsamic vinegar and onion and stir until well blended. Serve immediately over cooked trout.

Trout with Balsamic Basil Sauce
Omit green onions. Add 2 tablespoons minced fresh basil in step 3.

Trout with Balsamic Lemon Sauce
Add juice and grated zest of 1 lemon in step 3.

Grilled Tuna with Cilantro~Lime Butter

This easy butter-based sauce goes well with many types of grilled seafood, such as swordfish, shark or halibut. It also works well with chicken.

Servings: 4

4 ahi tuna steaks, about 6-8 oz. each

salt and freshly ground black pepper to taste

1/2 cup butter

grated zest of 1 lime

1 tablespoon minced fresh cilantro

1/4 cup freshly squeezed lime juice

Prepare a medium-hot grill.

1 Season tuna lightly with salt and pepper. Grill tuna steaks for about 10 to 12 minutes or until firm and opaque in the center. Transfer to a serving platter.

2 While tuna is grilling, melt butter in a small saucepan over medium heat.

3 Add lime zest, increase heat to high and bring butter just to the boiling point. Remove from heat and stir in cilantro. Keep warm.

4 Add lime juice to butter mixture and pour sauce over tuna steaks. Serve immediately.

Grilled Tuna with Parsley-Lemon Butter
Substitute lemon zest for lime zest and minced fresh parsley for cilantro in step 3. Substitute freshly squeezed lemon juice for lime juice in step 4.

Grilled Tuna with Caper-Lemon Butter
Substitute lemon zest for lime zest and 4 teaspoons drained capers for cilantro in step 3. Substitute freshly squeezed lemon juice for lime juice in step 4.

Entrées

Caribbean Chicken

The flavorful marinade used in this dish is similar to a jerk sauce, but not quite as hot. If you would like extra fire, add ½ seeded habanero chile.

Servings: 8

6 green onions, thinly sliced

½ yellow onion, minced

4 cloves garlic, minced

2 tablespoons minced peeled fresh ginger

2 tablespoons ground allspice

2 teaspoons freshly ground black pepper

2 teaspoons cinnamon

1 teaspoon freshly ground nutmeg

½ teaspoon salt

2 tablespoons dark brown sugar, packed

1 cup orange juice

¾ cup cider vinegar

½ cup soy sauce

2 tablespoons corn oil

8 boneless, skinless chicken breast halves

1 In a large nonmetallic bowl, combine green onions, yellow onion, garlic, ginger, allspice, pepper, cinnamon, nutmeg, salt, brown sugar, orange juice, vinegar, soy sauce and corn oil. Mix with a wire whisk until well blended.

2 Add chicken breasts and stir to coat well with marinade. Cover bowl and marinate chicken in the refrigerator for at least 8 hours.

3 Heat a grill to medium-low. Remove chicken from marinade. Transfer marinade to a small saucepan and bring to a boil; remove from heat.

4 Grill chicken for about 10 minutes, turning after 5 minutes, until cooked through, depending on thickness of breast. Baste breasts frequently with hot marinade while grilling. Serve hot.

Caribbean Spareribs
Substitute 4 lb. pork spareribs for chicken breasts in step 1.

Caribbean Pork Chops
Substitute 8 thick-cut boneless pork chops for chicken breasts in step 1.

Entrées

114

Chicken and Mushrooms with Mustard-Brandy Sauce

This dish is a staple in country French cooking. Substitute wild mushrooms instead of white mushrooms and you will add more sophistication in taste and texture to your meal.

Servings: 4

4 chicken breast halves

2 tablespoons butter

2 yellow onions, chopped

8 oz. sliced fresh white mushrooms

¼ cup brandy

¼ cup grainy mustard

1 cup heavy cream

1 In a large Dutch oven over medium heat, brown chicken on all sides, about 10 minutes per side. Remove chicken from pot and set aside.

2 Add butter to pot. When butter is melted, add onions and sauté until just beginning to brown. Add mushrooms and sauté until juices are released and evaporate.

3 Remove pot from heat and add brandy. Tilt pot and carefully ignite brandy with a long match (do not do this while an overhead fan or exhaust fan is running). Shake pot until flames disperse.

4 Add mustard and cream and stir well. Return chicken breasts to pot, cover and simmer over low heat for 15 minutes. Take care that sauce does not boil. Serve immediately on warm serving plates.

Chicken with Mustard-Brandy Sauce
Omit mushrooms.

Chicken with Mustard-Sherry Sauce
Omit mushrooms. Substitute dry sherry for brandy in step 3.

Chicken and Mushrooms with Brandy Sauce
Omit mustard.

Entrées

115

Stir-Fried Chicken with Two Onions

This recipe combines the flavors of a Chinese-style chicken stir-fry and French onion soup. The result is an easily prepared dish with unexpected flavors.

Servings: 4

1 teaspoon cornstarch

1 tablespoon dry sherry

3 boneless, skinless chicken breast halves, cut into thin slices

1 tablespoon vegetable oil

2 yellow onions, sliced

1/4 cup dry sherry

1 tablespoon Worcestershire sauce

3/4 cup chicken broth

2 tablespoons cornstarch

6 green onions, cut into 1-inch slices

1 In a medium bowl, stir together 1 teaspoon cornstarch and 1 tablespoon sherry. Add chicken and toss to coat evenly. Let stand for 15 minutes. Drain excess liquid from chicken.

2 Heat a large skillet or wok over high heat. Add oil. Add chicken mixture and stir-fry until chicken turns opaque. Add yellow onions and stir-fry just until onions soften and turn translucent.

3 In a small bowl, combine 1/4 cup sherry, Worcestershire sauce, chicken broth and 2 tablespoons cornstarch. Mix with a fork until smooth. Pour mixture over chicken and onions, stirring constantly.

4 Add green onions and stir-fry until sauce comes to a boil and thickens. Serve immediately.

Stir-Fried Beef with Two Onions
Substitute 2 cups sliced beef for chicken in step 1.

Stir-Fried Chicken with Wine and Two Onions
Substitute white wine for sherry in steps 1 and 3.

Stir-Fried Chicken with Yellow Onions
Omit green onions.

Grilled Chicken Breasts with Outback Salsa

Fruit salsas lend an intriguing combination of sweet and savory flavors to grilled chicken breasts. Add your choice of hot peppers to give the dish a touch of fire.

Servings: 4

4 chicken breasts

1 cup pineapple juice

¼ cup freshly squeezed lime juice

6 kiwi fruit, peeled and coarsely chopped

2/3 cup chopped red onion

2 jalapeño peppers, seeded and minced

2 teaspoons light brown sugar

1 In a large nonmetalic dish, combine chicken breasts, pineapple juice and 2 tablespoons of lime juice. Cover and let stand at room temperature for 30 minutes or in a refrigerator for up to 4 hours.

2 Heat a grill to medium. Grill chicken breasts for about 30 to 40 minutes until cooked through, turning occasionally.

3 While chicken is cooking, combine kiwi fruit, onion, jalapeños, remaining 2 tablespoons lime juice and brown sugar in a nonmetalic bowl. Stir until well mixed.

4 Place grilled chicken on a serving platter. Spoon salsa over chicken and serve immediately.

Grilled Chicken Breasts with Volcano Salsa

Substitute 2 cups chopped fresh pineapple for kiwi in step 3. Add ¼ teaspoon crushed dried red chile peppers to salsa in step 3.

Grilled Chicken Breasts with Caribbean Salsa

Substitute 2 peeled, seeded, coarsely chopped fresh papayas for kiwi in step 3. Add ¼ teaspoon ground allspice to salsa in step 3.

Entrées

Braised Chicken with Artichokes and Tomatoes

This is a traditional Northern Italian presentation of a chicken stew. Try it served over polenta or tiny pasta to soak up the delicious sauce.

Servings: 6~8

1 tablespoon olive oil

1 chicken, 3 lb., cut into serving pieces

1 yellow onion, sliced

2 cloves garlic, minced

2 cups artichoke hearts

1 cup dry white wine

2 cups chopped tomatoes

1/2 teaspoon salt

1 In a large skillet, heat oil over medium heat. Add chicken pieces and brown on all sides.

2 Remove chicken from skillet and set aside. Add onion and garlic and sauté until they begin to brown.

3 Add artichoke hearts, white wine, tomatoes and salt and bring mixture to a boil. Add chicken pieces.

4 Cover skillet, reduce heat to low and simmer for 15 minutes, until chicken is cooked through. Serve immediately.

Braised Chicken Breasts with Artichokes and Tomatoes
Substitute 4 large chicken breasts for chicken pieces in step 1.

Braised Chicken with White Wine and Artichokes
Omit tomatoes. Add 1 cup chicken broth in step 3.

Roasted Chicken with Fresh Sage

Fresh sage and dry white wine pair well together with a recipe for a classic roasted chicken dinner.

Servings: 6~8

1 tablespoon finely minced fresh sage

½ cup butter, softened

½ teaspoon salt

1 roasting chicken, cut into serving pieces

½ cup dry white wine

Preheat oven to 375°.

1 In a small bowl, combine sage, softened butter and salt. Stir until well mixed.

2 Rub butter mixture over the surface of all chicken pieces. Arrange chicken in a 9-x-13-inch baking dish.

3 Bake for 30 minutes. Pour wine over chicken and bake for 10 additional minutes. Transfer chicken to a platter. Remove fat from the surface of pan juices and strain pan juices into a serving dish. Serve chicken with pan juices.

Roasted Chicken with Fresh Sage and Lemon
Add juice of 1 lemon with wine in step 3.

Roasted Chicken with Fresh Thyme
Substitute minced fresh thyme for sage in step 1.

Roasted Chicken with Chervil
Substitute minced fresh chervil for sage in step 1.

Entrées

119

Roasted Chicken with Rice~Walnut Stuffing

Nuts and rice are a simple, yet rich~tasting combination. Here they are used as a stuffing for an easy~to~prepare roasted chicken.

Servings: 6~8

2 tablespoons butter

1 yellow onion, chopped

3/4 cup chopped walnuts

1/4 teaspoon ground thyme

1/4 teaspoon ground sage

1 teaspoon salt

2 1/2 cups cooked white rice

1 roasting chicken, 5 lb.

2 tablespoons walnut oil

5-6 cups chicken broth

1/4 cup all-purpose flour

Preheat oven to 325°.

1. In a medium skillet, melt butter over medium heat. Add onion and sauté until translucent.

2. Add walnuts and sauté until onion begins to brown and walnuts are toasted.

3. Remove skillet from heat and stir in thyme, sage, salt and cooked rice. Set aside.

4. Remove giblets from chicken and rinse surface and cavity with cold running water. Drain well and pat skin dry with paper towels. Place chicken on a work surface.

5. Spoon rice mixture loosely into body cavity and tie legs together with kitchen string to hold stuffing inside.

6. Rub outside of chicken with walnut oil. Place chicken in a roasting pan. Roast for 2 1/2 to 3 hours, or until a thermometer reads 180°~185° when inserted into the thickest part of thigh. Baste chicken frequently with broth during roasting.

7. Transfer chicken to a serving platter. Pour 4 cups of pan drippings into a 4~cup measuring cup. Add chicken broth if necessary until it measures 4 cups. Pour mixture into a medium saucepan. Sprinkle flour over mixture and mix well with a wire whisk.

8 Bring gravy to a boil over high heat, stirring constantly. Reduce heat to low and simmer for 5 minutes, stirring frequently until thickened. Strain gravy through a sieve and transfer to a gravy boat.

9 With a large spoon, remove stuffing from chicken cavity and place on a warm serving plate. Carve chicken into serving pieces and serve with stuffing and gravy.

Roasted Chicken with Rice~Hazelnut Stuffing

Substitute chopped hazelnuts for walnuts in step 2. Substitute vegetable oil for walnut oil in step 6.

Roasted Chicken with Rice~Cashew Stuffing

Substitute cashew pieces for walnuts in step 2. Substitute vegetable oil for walnut oil in step 6.

Chipotle Pork Stew

Chipotle peppers, otherwise known as smoked jalapeños, are both hot and smoky. They add fire to this pork dish and a subtle smoky flavor. You can intensify the heat and smoke by adding more peppers. Always rehydrate the chipotles before attempting to remove the seeds and ribs. Look for dried chipotle peppers in a Latin American market or specialty food store.

Servings: 6

1 tablespoon vegetable oil

2 lb. boneless pork pieces

1/2 cup boiling water

3 dried chipotle peppers

1 can (15 oz.) peeled tomatoes

2 cups chicken broth

1 yellow onion, chopped

2 cloves garlic, minced

1/2 teaspoon ground cumin

1/2 teaspoon salt

1 In a large pot, heat oil over medium heat. Add pork and sauté until pork begins to brown, about 15 minutes.

2 While pork is cooking, combine boiling water and chipotles in a small bowl and let stand for 15 minutes. Drain peppers, reserving water, and remove seeds and ribs. Coarsely chop peppers.

3 Add reserved chipotle liquid, chopped chipotles, tomatoes, chicken broth, onion, garlic, cumin and salt to pan with browned pork. Bring mixture to a boil over high heat. Reduce heat to low and simmer uncovered for 2 hours or until pork is fork-tender and sauce is thickened and reduced. Serve hot.

Chipotle Pork and Vegetable Stew
Add 1 1/2 cups chopped carrots and 1 1/2 cups cubed potatoes with tomatoes in step 3.

Saucy Chipotle Pork Ribs
Substitute 4 lb. pork spareribs for boneless pork in step 1.

Honey~Mustard Pork Tenderloin

Y ou can also prepare this dish by grilling the pork and then bast~ing with the honey mustard sauce in the final minutes of grilling. The smoky flavor of grilling accents the sweetness of the honey. When basting any meat with a sweet sauce, make sure to keep the meat over very low or indirect heat to prevent burning.

Servings: 4

1 pork tenderloin, 2 lb.

½ cup apple juice

½ cup grainy mustard

½ cup honey

Preheat oven to 325°. Spray a 9-x-13-inch baking dish with nonstick cooking spray.

1 Cut pork tenderloin into 8 thick slices and place in a shallow dish with ⅓ cup of the apple juice. Let mixture stand at room temperature for 30 minutes, turning once.

2 In a small bowl, combine mustard, honey and remaining apple juice. Remove pork from apple juice and pat dry. Rub mustard mixture over pork slices and place in prepared baking dish. Cover dish tightly with foil.

3 Bake pork for 30 minutes or until cooked through. Serve immediately.

Maple~Mustard Pork Tenderloin
Substitute ½ cup maple syrup for honey in step 2.

Orange~Mustard Pork Tenderloin
Substitute freshly squeezed orange juice for apple juice in steps 1 and 2.

Entrées

123

Pork Chops with Orange~Bourbon Sauce

This sauce dresses up ordinary old pork chops for a weekend family repast or special company dinner.

Servings: 6~8

1 tablespoon vegetable oil

4 thick-cut boneless pork chops

½ cup bourbon

1 cup orange juice

2 tablespoons honey

1 lb. sweet potatoes, peeled and thickly sliced

If the month has been especially profitable, consider purchasing a distinguished bottle of bourbon. Blanton's, Baker's, or Maker's Mark are all fine choices.

1 In a large skillet, heat oil over medium heat. Add pork chops and brown lightly on both sides, about 10 minutes per side. Remove from pan and set aside.

2 Remove pan from heat and pour out any excess fat. Add bourbon to pan. Tilt pan and carefully ignite bourbon using a long match (do not attempt this while an overhead fan or exhaust fan is running). Shake pot until flames disperse.

3 Add orange juice and honey to skillet and bring to a boil over high heat. Reduce heat to low and add potatoes. Place pork chops on top of potatoes.

4 Cover skillet and simmer until potatoes are tender, about 20 minutes depending on thickness of potatoes. Serve immediately on warm serving plates.

Pork Chops with Orange Sauce
Omit bourbon.

Pork Chops and Apples with Orange~Bourbon Sauce
Arrange 2 sliced Granny Smith apples on top of pork chops in step 3 and continue with recipe.

Italian Beef Stew

F or a traditional Italian presentation, spoon this stew over cooked polenta. It is even better the next day!

Servings: 6~8

Ingredients:

2 tablespoons olive oil

1 yellow onion, chopped

2 cloves garlic, minced

2 lb. beef stew meat

1/2 cup chopped fresh Italian parsley

4 cups coarsely chopped peeled Roma tomatoes

1 cup dry red wine

2 cups beef broth

1/4 teaspoon freshly ground black pepper

1/4 teaspoon cinnamon

1/2 teaspoon salt

1. In a large pot, heat olive oil over medium-high heat. Add onion and garlic and sauté until onion is translucent.

2. Add beef and increase heat to high. Sauté beef mixture until beef just begins to brown.

3. Add parsley, tomatoes, wine, broth, pepper, cinnamon and salt and bring mixture to a boil over high heat. Reduce heat to low and simmer uncovered for 2 hours or until beef is fork-tender.

Italian Beef Stew with Vegetables
About 45 minutes before serving, add 2 medium zucchini (thickly sliced), 2 carrots (peeled and thickly sliced) and 1 1/2 cups 2-inch-long fresh green bean pieces.

Herbed Italian Beef Stew
Omit cinnamon. Add 1 teaspoon dried oregano and 1 teaspoon dried basil with seasonings in step 3.

Beef Roast with Winter Vegetables

Changing vegetables in recipes can give you dramatically different results. Here, a beef roast can be presented at any time of the year, depending on the vegetables that are available.

Servings: 8

1 tablespoon vegetable oil

1 rib-eye roast, 4 lb.

3½ cups beef broth

5 black peppercorns

1 bay leaf

1 clove garlic, chopped

1 teaspoon salt

8 small potatoes, cut in half

8 carrots, peeled and cut in half

2 yellow onions, peeled and cut into quarters

4 turnips, peeled and cut into quarters

¼ cup all-purpose flour

Preheat oven to 325°.

1 In a large Dutch oven, heat oil over medium heat. Add beef roast and brown on all sides.

2 Add 1 cup of the beef broth, peppercorns, bay leaf, garlic and salt to pot. Bring mixture to a boil. Cover pot, transfer to oven and bake for 2½ hours.

3 Add potatoes, carrots, onions and turnips to pot and bake covered for an additional 45 to 60 minutes or until beef and vegetables are tender.

4 Transfer beef and vegetables to a serving platter; keep warm while preparing gravy.

5 Skim excess fat from pan drippings and pour 2 cups drippings into a measuring cup. Add additional beef broth to equal 2 cups. Pour mixture into a small saucepan.

6 In a small bowl, whisk together flour and ½ cup beef broth until smooth. Gradually stir flour mixture into broth mixture and mix well until smooth.

7 Heat gravy over medium heat, stirring constantly. Bring gravy to a boil for 1 minute, stirring constantly. Serve with beef and vegetables.

Beef Roast with Spring Vegetables

Omit potatoes, carrots, onions and turnips. In step 2, bake roast for 3 hours. In step 3, add 1/2 lb. trimmed whole baby zucchini or other baby squash, 1/2 lb. trimmed whole baby carrots and 8 green onions, cut into quarters. Cover and continue to bake for an additional 1/2 hour.

Beef Roast with Autumn Vegetables

Omit potatoes, carrots, onions and turnips. In step 2, add 6 halved Yukon Gold potatoes, 1 lb. 2-inch chunks butternut squash and 2 quartered yellow bell peppers.

Garlic Beef Provençal with Leeks

You will love the way your home smells as this beef roasts in your oven. Serve it with your favorite roasted potatoes and a smooth red wine.

Servings: 8

1 tablespoon olive oil

1 beef roast, 3-4 lb.

6 cloves garlic, sliced

2 cups sliced leeks

1½ teaspoons fresh thyme leaves

1 cup dry red wine

1 teaspoon salt

½ teaspoon freshly ground black pepper

2 bay leaves

¼ cup beef broth

3 tablespoons all-purpose flour

Preheat oven to 325°.

1 In a large Dutch oven, heat oil over medium heat. Add beef roast and brown evenly on all sides.

2 Add garlic, leeks, thyme, red wine, salt, pepper and bay leaves. Cover and bake for 2½ to 3 hours or until meat is fork-tender. Transfer meat to a cutting board and let stand for 10 minutes.

3 Strain sauce, reserving leek, garlic and herbs. Pour strained sauce into a small saucepan. Bring sauce to a boil over medium-high heat. Mix together beef broth and flour until smooth. Slowly stir flour mixture into boiling sauce, stirring constantly. Reduce heat to medium and cook for 5 minutes, stirring constantly. Return leeks, garlic and herbs to thickened sauce.

4 Slice beef against the grain and place on a serving platter. Pour leek sauce over sliced beef and serve immediately.

Garlic Beef Provençal
Omit leeks.

Garlic Beef Provençal with Onions
Substitute 1 cup thinly sliced yellow onion for
leeks in step 2.

Beef Provençal
Reduce garlic to 1 clove in step 2.

Mexican Flank Steak

Flank steak absorbs flavors well. With a simple rub, this grilled steak becomes very juicy and flavorful.

Servings: 4

juice of 2 limes

2 teaspoon ground cumin

1/2 teaspoon cayenne pepper

1/2 teaspoon freshly ground black pepper

2 tablespoons sliced green onions

1 clove garlic, minced

1 lb. flank steak

1 In a small bowl, combine lime juice, cumin, cayenne, black pepper, green onions and garlic. Stir until mixture forms a thin paste.

2 Rub paste over both sides of flank steak. Place meat on a platter and cover with plastic wrap. Refrigerate for 4 hours.

3 Prepare a medium-hot grill. Grill meat to desired doneness. To serve, slice against the grain and arrange on a platter.

Mexican Flank Steak with Peppers
Core and seed 1 green and 1 red bell pepper. Cut peppers into quarters. Place peppers on grill with meat and cook until tender-crisp. Serve grilled peppers with sliced flank steak.

Mexican Flank Steak with Smoky Onions
Cut 2 yellow onions into 4 thick rings each. Place onions on grilled meat and cook until charred on each side. Serve charred, grilled onions with sliced flank steak.

Pan-Seared Filet Mignon with Brie Sauce

This is the recipe to go off your diet for! Tender beef needs only a simple Brie sauce to show off its flavors. The variations let you experiment with other rich cheeses.

Servings: 4

¼ cup butter

4 filet mignon steaks, 1½ inches thick

½ cup heavy cream

½ cup Brie cheese, rind removed

¼ teaspoon freshly ground black pepper

1 In a large skillet, heat butter over medium-high heat. Add steaks and cook until evenly browned, about 2 minutes on each side for rare and about 3 minutes on each side for medium. Transfer steaks to a serving platter and keep warm.

2 Reduce heat to medium-low and add cream, Brie and pepper to skillet. Cook, stirring constantly, until Brie is melted and sauce is hot; make sure that mixture does not boil. Spoon hot sauce over steaks and serve immediately.

Pan-Seared Filet Mignon with Herbed Brie Sauce
Substitute herbed Brie cheese for regular Brie in step 2.

Pan-Seared Filet Mignon with Peppercorn Brie Sauce
Substitute peppered Brie cheese for regular Brie in step 2.

Pan-Seared Filet Mignon with Gorgonzola Sauce
Substitute crumbled Gorgonzola cheese for Brie cheese in step 2.

Grilled Filet Mignon with Chile Butter

Good cuts of beef seldom need more than a touch of sauce to accent their flavors. The beef is marinated with red wine and topped with a touch of rich-flavored butter.

Servings: 4

1 cup dry red wine

2 tablespoons balsamic vinegar

½ teaspoon freshly ground black pepper

1 clove garlic, finely minced

4 filet mignon steaks

¼ cup butter, softened

⅛ teaspoon crushed dried red chiles

¼ teaspoon ground cumin

⅛ teaspoon cayenne pepper

1 In a shallow nonmetallic baking dish, combine wine, vinegar, pepper and garlic; stir until mixed. Add steaks to marinade, cover and let stand for 30 minutes at room temperature or up to 4 hours in the refrigerator.

2 While steaks are marinating, combine butter, chiles, cumin and cayenne pepper in a small bowl. Mix until well blended and set aside.

3 Broil or grill steaks to desired doneness and place steaks on a serving platter. Place 1 tablespoon chile butter on each steak and serve immediately.

Grilled Filet Mignon
with Blue Cheese Butter
Omit chiles, cumin and cayenne. Add ¼ cup crumbled blue cheese to butter mixture in step 2.

Filet Mignon with Garlic Herb Butter
Omit chiles, cumin and cayenne. Add 1 clove garlic, minced and 1 teaspoon minced fresh chives to butter mixture in step 2.

Desserts

Desserts

Nutty Biscotti 140
Pine Nut Biscotti
Walnut Biscotti
Almond Biscotti

Biscotti Crumbles 141
Oatmeal Crumbles
Shortbread Crumbles
Nutty Biscotti Crumbles

Chocolate Chip Cookies 142
Chocolate-Chip Walnut Cookies
White Chocolate-Macadamia Cookies
Butterfinger Chip Cookies

Oatmeal Raisin Cookies 143
Oatmeal-Raisin Walnut Cookies
Cinnamon-Oatmeal Raisin Cookies
Oatmeal Cookies
Fruity Oatmeal Cookies

Lemon Cookies 144
Lemon Coconut Cookies
Citrus Confetti Cookies
Vanilla Cream Cheese Cookies

Blackberry Bars 145
Raspberry Bars
Strawberry Bars

Mixed Berry Cobbler 146
Orange-Scented Berry Cobbler
Peach-Berry Cobbler

Spiced Blackberry Pie 147
Spiced Apple-Blackberry Pie
Blackberry Pie

Vanilla Almond Snow Pie 148
Vanilla Snow Pie
Peppermint Snow Pie

Mocha Mud Pie 149
Chocolate Mud Pie
Cappuccino Mud Pie

White Chocolate Sin 150
Milk Chocolate Sin
Bittersweet Chocolate Sin

California Strawberry Shortcakes 152
Lemon and Berry Shortcakes
Mixed Berry Shortcakes

Bittersweet Chocolate Cake 154
Bittersweet Chocolate Layer Cake
Bittersweet Chocolate and Walnut Cake
Dark Chocolate Cake

Fresh Apple Walnut Cake 155
Apple Cake
Apple Spice Cake

Chocolate Walnut Torte 156
Chocolate Almond Torte
Chocolate Hazelnut Torte

Butter Cake 157
Chocolate Chip Butter Cake
Chocolate Chip-Nut Butter Cake

Banana Bread Pudding 158
Banana Honey Bread Pudding
Spiced Banana Bread Pudding
Chocolate Chip Banana Bread Pudding
Banana-Raisin Bread Pudding

Glazed Pears with Cardamom Cream 159
Glazed Pears with Cinammon Cream
Glazed Pears with Ginger Cream
Glazed Pears with Nutmeg Cream

Lemon Mousse 160
Orange Mousse
Blood Orange Mousse
Lime Mousse
Citrus Mousse

Pear Clafouti 162
Pear-Blueberry Clafouti
Pear-Raspberry Clafouti
Peach Clafouti

Classic Crème Brulée 163
Blackberry Crème Brulée
Coffee Crème Brulée

Vanilla Intensity Gelato 164
Honey-Vanilla Gelato
Vanilla-Chocolate Chunk Gelato
Vanilla-Almond Gelato

Cappuccino Gelato 165
Caf au Lait Gelato
Flavored Coffee Gelato

Coconut Ice Cream 166
Toasted Coconut Ice Cream
Coconut-Macadamia Ice Cream

Fresh Raspberry Sorbet 167
Fresh Blackberry Sorbet
Fresh Strawberry Sorbet
Fresh Strawberry and Grand Marnier
  Sorbet

Raspberry Sauce 168
Blackberry Sauce
Strawberry Sauce

Nutty Biscotti

These biscotti are not quite as hard and dry as those you can pur~ chase and are still delicious when you dip them into your espres~ so in the morning.

Makes 36 Cookies

2/3 cup unsalted butter

1 1/2 cups sugar

4 eggs

1 tablespoon vanilla extract

4 1/2 cups all- purpose flour

1 tablespoon baking powder

1/2 teaspoon salt

1 cup chopped pecans

Preheat oven to 325°. Grease and flour a baking sheet.

1 In a bowl, mix butter and sugar with a mixer until light and fluffy. Add eggs and vanilla extract and beat until well mixed.

2 Add flour, baking powder, salt and pecans and mix until dough is well blended.

3 Remove dough from bowl and divide into 4 equal portions. Shape each portion into a log about 12 inches long. Place logs on a baking sheet about 2 inches apart. Bake for 25 to 30 minutes or until logs are just beginning to brown.

4 Cool logs for 10 minutes. Cut logs into diagonal slices about 1/2-inch thick. Lay slices flat on baking sheet.

5 Bake slices for 5 minutes. Turn and bake until golden, about 5 more minutes. Cool on a rack.

Pine Nut Biscotti
Substitute pine nuts for pecans in step 2.

Walnut Biscotti
Substitute walnuts for pecans in step 2.

Almond Biscotti
Substitute slivered almonds for pecans in step 2.

Biscotti Crumbles

Think of these as dessert croutons. They can top your favorite ice cream or gelato or be sprinkled over fresh fruit. The biscotti should be crumbled into pieces the size of small croutons.

Makes 2 Cups Crumbles

¼ cup butter

2 cups crumbled plain biscotti

¼ teaspoon cinnamon

1 In a medium saucepan, heat butter over medium heat until melted.

2 Add crumbled biscotti and cinnamon and stir until evenly coated. Cook, stirring, until biscotti are golden brown, about 10 minutes.

3 Cool mixture and store in a covered container in the refrigerator until ready to use.

Oatmeal Crumbles
Substitute crumbled plain oatmeal cookies for biscotti in step 2.

Shortbread Crumbles
Substitute crumbled plain Scotch shortbread or plain sugar cookies for biscotti in step 2.

Nutty Biscotti Crumbles
Substitute crumbled biscotti with nuts for plain biscotti in step 2.

Chocolate Chip Cookies

There are many recipes for chocolate chip cookies and each version is a bit different. This recipe yields a soft, chewy cookie with lots of options for personalized variations.

Makes 48 Cookies

1 cup butter, softened

1 cup light brown sugar, packed

1/2 cup granulated sugar

2 eggs

2 teaspoons vanilla extract

2¾ cups all-purpose flour

1 teaspoon baking soda

1 teaspoon salt

1 pkg. (12 oz.) semisweet chocolate chips

Preheat oven to 325°.

1 In a large bowl, combine butter, brown sugar and granulated sugar. Mix with a mixer until light and fluffy. Add eggs and vanilla and mix until well blended.

2 Add flour, baking soda and salt and mix until dough is well blended.

3 Add chocolate chips and stir with a wooden spoon until well mixed.

4 Drop dough by rounded tablespoonfuls onto an ungreased baking sheet. Bake until golden, about 12 minutes. Cool on a baking sheet for 5 minutes. Transfer cookies to a rack to cool completely.

Chocolate Chip-Walnut Cookies
Stir in 1 cup chopped walnuts in step 3.

White Chocolate-Macadamia Cookies
Substitute white chocolate chips for chocolate chips and add 1 cup chopped macadamia nuts in step 3.

Butterfinger Chip Cookies
Substitute 2 Butterfinger candy bars, coarsely chopped, for chocolate chips in step 3.

Oatmeal Raisin Cookies

Soft and chewy with lots of raisins, these cookies are destined to become one of your favorites. They are very easy to modify by using different dried fruits and nuts.

Makes 48 Cookies

1 cup butter, softened

1 cup light brown sugar, packed

1/2 cup granulated sugar

2 eggs

1 teaspoon vanilla extract

2 cups quick-cooking oats

1 1/2 cups all-purpose flour

1 teaspoon baking soda

1 teaspoon salt

1 cup raisins

Preheat oven to 350°.

1 In a bowl, mix butter, brown sugar and granulated sugar until light and fluffy. Add eggs and vanilla extract and mix until well blended.

2 Add oatmeal, flour, baking soda and salt and mix until dough is well blended.

3 Add raisins and stir with a wooden spoon until well distributed.

4 Drop dough by rounded tablespoonfuls onto an ungreased baking sheet. Bake until golden, about 12 minutes. Cool on baking sheet for 5 minutes. Transfer cookies to a rack to cool completely.

Oatmeal-Raisin Walnut Cookies
Add 1 cup chopped walnuts in step 3.

Cinnamon-Oatmeal Raisin Cookies
Add 1/2 teaspoon freshly ground cinnamon in step 2.

Oatmeal Cookies
Omit step 3.

Fruity Oatmeal Cookies
Substitute sweetened dried cranberries or chopped dried apples, apricots or pears for raisins in step 3.

Desserts

143

Lemon Cookies

Thece little cookies have a big rich taste. They're wonderful served with tea or evening coffee.

Makes 36 Cookies

1 cup butter, softened

8 oz. cream cheese, softened

2 cups sugar

1 teaspoon lemon extract

1 teaspoon grated fresh lemon zest

2 cups all-purpose flour

1 In a large bowl, mix butter and cream cheese with a mixer until light and fluffy. Add sugar, lemon extract and lemon zest and mix until creamy.

2 Add flour and mix until dough is well blended. Remove dough from bowl and form into a ball.

3 Cover dough with plastic wrap and refrigerate for at least 2 hours.

4 Preheat oven to 350°. Roll dough between your hands to form balls about the size of a ping pong ball. Place balls about 2 inches apart on an ungreased baking sheet.

5 Bake cookies until edges just begin to brown, about 12 to 14 minutes. Transfer cookies to a wire rack to cool completely. Store in an airtight container.

Lemon Coconut Cookies
Add 1/2 cup flaked coconut in step 2.

Citrus Confetti Cookies
Substitute 3/4 teaspoon grated fresh orange zest and 1/2 teaspoon grated fresh lime zest for lemon zest in step 1.

Vanilla Cream Cheese Cookies
Omit lemon extract and lemon zest. Add 2 teaspoons vanilla extract in step 1.

Blackberry Bars

Although these are cookies, they are healthy enough to be served as breakfast bars. And they're low in fat, too! Store uneaten bars in an airtight container.

Makes 24 Cookies

2½ cups fresh or frozen blackberries

1 tablespoon cornstarch

½ cup granulated sugar

¾ cup butter

1 cup brown sugar, packed

3 eggs

1½ cups whole wheat flour

¾ cup wheat germ, toasted

1½ teaspoons baking soda

¾ teaspoon salt

2¼ cups quick-cooking oats

Preheat oven to 375°. Spray the bottom and sides of a 9-x-12-inch baking pan with nonstick cooking spray.

1 In a medium saucepan, combine blackberries, cornstarch and sugar and stir until well mixed. Cook over medium heat, stirring frequently until berries collapse and juices are released. Continue to cook until mixture thickens and coats the back of a spoon. Cool and set aside.

2 With a mixer, mix butter and brown sugar until light and creamy. Add eggs and mix for 1 minute. In another bowl, stir together flour, wheat germ, baking soda, salt and oats. Add flour mixture to butter mixture and stir with a spoon until dough is thoroughly blended.

3 Divide dough mixture in half. Press half into prepared pan evenly. Pour berry mixture over the top and gently spread to within ¼ inch of the edge. Gently crumble remaining half of dough over berry mixture.

4 Bake until edges are lightly browned, about 20 minutes. Cool in pan and cut into 3-x-3-inch bars.

Raspberry Bars
Substitute fresh or frozen raspberries for blackberries in step 1.

Strawberry Bars
Substitute fresh or frozen strawberries for blackberries in step 1.

Mixed Berry Cobbler

Fruit cobblers are easy and delicious. Combining different fruits into a cobbler compliments fruit flavors and is a great use for any summer fruit that is in abundance.

Servings: 6~8

2 cups fresh blackberries

2 cups fresh raspberries

1 cup fresh blueberries

½ cup sugar

1 tablespoon cornstarch

1 cup all-purpose flour

1 tablespoon sugar

1½ teaspoons baking powder

½ teaspoon salt

3 tablespoons butter

½ cup milk

Preheat oven to 375°.

1 In a large bowl, combine blackberries, raspberries, blueberries, sugar and cornstarch and toss gently until mixed. Transfer mixture to an 8-x-8-inch baking dish.

2 In a medium bowl, combine flour, sugar, baking powder and salt. With a pastry blender or two knives, cut in butter until mixture resembles fine crumbs. Stir in milk and mix just until mixture is moistened.

3 Drop dough over berry mixture in baking dish, distributing evenly over berries.

4 Bake until topping is golden brown and berry mixture is bubbling, about 30 to 35 minutes. Serve warm.

Orange~Scented Berry Cobbler
Omit blueberries. Increase blackberries to 3 cups. Add 1 tablespoon grated fresh orange zest in step 1.

Peach~Berry Cobbler
Omit blueberries. Add 2 cups peeled sliced peaches in step 1.

Spiced Blackberry Pie

Frozen blackberries are readily available, which make this pie perfect for summer or winter. The spicy flavors make this pie a great finish to a holiday meal.

Servings: 6

pastry for one 9-inch double-crust pie

6 cups fresh blackberries or frozen blackberries, thawed

3/4 cup sugar

1/4 cup all-purpose flour

3/4 teaspoon cinnamon

1/4 teaspoon ground nutmeg

1/4 teaspoon ground allspice

Preheat oven to 425°.

1 Line a 9-inch pie pan with one of the pie crusts. Reserve remaining pie crust.

2 In a large bowl, combine berries, sugar, flour, cinnamon, nutmeg and allspice and toss until well mixed. Pour berry mixture into crust-lined pie pan. Roll out reserved pie crust slightly and position on top of filling.

3 Bake for about 45 minutes, until bubbling and golden brown. If crust begins to brown too quickly, cover pie with a sheet of aluminum foil while baking. Cool pie slightly and serve warm. Or, cool completely and serve at room temperature.

Spiced Apple-Blackberry Pie
Reduce blackberries to 3 cups. Add 3 cups sliced, peeled Pippin apples in step 2.

Blackberry Pie
Omit any or all of the spices from step 2.

Desserts

Vanilla Almond Snow Pie

Here's a festive take on a traditional mud pie. Almond-flavored ice cream and a vanilla wafer crust pair wonderfully.

Servings: 6

3 eggs

1 cup sugar

2 cups milk

1 teaspoon
vanilla extract

1 teaspoon
almond extract

1/2 cup
sliced almonds

2 cups
heavy cream

1 prepared vanilla
wafer pie crust

1 In a medium saucepan, combine eggs and sugar and stir until well mixed. Add milk and mix well.

2 Cook mixture over medium heat, stirring constantly until it thickens and coats the back of a spoon, about 15 minutes.

3 Cool mixture slightly and transfer to a covered container. Refrigerate mixture for at least 4 hours or until very cold.

4 Stir mixture until smooth. Add vanilla extract, almond extract, sliced almonds and cream, stirring until well mixed. Transfer mixture to an ice cream maker and freeze according to manufacturer's directions.

5 When frozen, transfer ice cream to vanilla pie crust. Cover pie with plastic wrap and freeze until firm, about 3 hours. To serve, let pie stand at room temperature for about 5 to 10 minutes before cutting into wedges.

Vanilla Snow Pie
Omit almond extract and almonds. Increase vanilla extract to 1 tablespoon in step 4.

Peppermint Snow Pie
Omit almond extract and almonds. Add 1 teaspoon peppermint extract and 1/2 cup crushed peppermint candies in step 4.

Mocha Mud Pie

Mud pie is even more of a treat when you make it with home-made ice cream. Top it with your favorite chocolate sauce and whipped cream.

Servings: 6

3 eggs

1 cup sugar

2 cups milk

two 1 oz. squares unsweetened chocolate

1 tablespoon instant coffee

1 teaspoon vanilla extract

2 cups heavy cream

1 prepared chocolate wafer pie crust

1 In a medium saucepan, combine eggs and sugar and stir until well mixed. Add milk and mix well.

2 Cook mixture over medium heat, stirring constantly until it thickens and coats the back of a spoon, about 15 minutes.

3 Melt chocolate in a microwave or in a saucepan over low heat. Add to egg mixture and mix well. Add instant coffee and stir until coffee is dissolved and mixture is smooth. Cool mixture slightly and transfer to a covered container. Refrigerate mixture for at least 4 hours or until very cold.

4 Stir mixture until smooth. Add vanilla extract and cream, stirring until well mixed. Transfer mixture to an ice cream maker and freeze according to manufacturer's directions.

5 When frozen, transfer ice cream to chocolate pie crust. Cover pie with plastic wrap and freeze until firm, about 3 hours. To serve, let pie stand at room temperature for about 5 to 10 minutes before cutting into wedges.

Chocolate Mud Pie
Omit coffee.

Cappuccino Mud Pie
Omit chocolate. Increase instant coffee to 1/4 cup in step 3.

White Chocolate Sin

White chocolate plus butter and sugar equals pure sin. This is a very sweet and rich dessert; try serving it with a tart berry sauce to offset the sweetness.

Servings: 8-10

1 cup white
chocolate chips

1/2 cup butter

3 eggs

1 cup sugar

1/2 teaspoon
vanilla extract

3/4 cup all-
purpose flour

fresh raspberries or
blackberries, optional

Preheat oven to 350°. Spray the bottom and sides of a 9-inch springform pan with nonstick cooking spray.

1 In a small saucepan, combine white chocolate and butter. Cook over low heat, stirring until mixture is melted and smooth.

2 In a large bowl, combine eggs, sugar and vanilla. Beat with an electric mixer on high speed for 2 minutes. Reduce mixer speed to low and slowly pour in chocolate mixture. Mix until thoroughly blended.

3 Add flour and mix with a wooden spoon until just incorporated. Transfer mixture to prepared pan

4 Bake until the center is firm to the touch and the top is golden, about 35 minutes. Cool on a wire rack. Serve at room temperature with berries, if desired.

Milk Chocolate Sin
Substitute milk chocolate chips for white chocolate chips in step 1.

Bittersweet Chocolate Sin
Substitute bittersweet chocolate chips for white
chocolate chips in step 1.

California Strawberry Shortcakes

Real shortcakes are a type of biscuit, not at all like the sponge cake shortcakes available at the supermarket. The biscuit absorbs some of the juices and creates a nice contrast to the ripe berries.

Servings: 4

2 tablespoons sugar

2 cups plus 2 tablespoons all-purpose flour

2 teaspoons baking powder

1 teaspoon salt

5 tablespoons vegetable shortening

grated zest of 1 orange

¾ cup milk

2 cups sliced fresh strawberries

¼ cup sugar

1 tablespoon Grand Marnier, optional

whipped cream

Preheat oven to 425°.

1 In a large bowl, sift sugar, flour, baking powder and salt.

2 With a pastry blender or two knives, cut in shortening until mixture resembles coarse crumbs.

3 Add orange zest and milk. Stir just until mixture forms a soft dough that leaves the sides of bowl.

4 Transfer dough to a lightly floured surface. Knead dough 6 or 8 times to mix thoroughly.

5 Roll out dough to a ¾-inch-thick round. With a floured 2-inch biscuit cutter, cut dough and place on an ungreased baking sheet.

6 Bake until light golden brown, about 12 to 18 minutes. Cool on a rack.

7 In a bowl, mix strawberries, sugar and Grand Marnier, if using, and let stand for 30 minutes.

8 Slice shortcakes in half and place bottom half on a plate. Top each shortcake half with a spoonful of strawberry mixture and whipped cream. Place remaining shortcake half on top. Serve immediately.

Lemon and Berry Shortcakes

Substitute the grated zest of 1 lemon for orange zest in step 3. Omit Grand Mariner. Substitute 2 cups fresh or frozen blackberries for strawberries in step 7.

Mixed Berry Shortcakes

Reduce strawberries to 1 cup. Add 1/2 cup fresh blueberries and 1/2 cup blackberries or raspberries in step 7.

Bittersweet Chocolate Cake

This is a cake that everyone loves. If desired, you can frost this cake with cream cheese frosting or your favorite chocolate frosting flavored with 1 teaspoon rum extract.

Servings: 8-10

1/2 cup butter

1¼ cups sugar

3 eggs

3/4 cup milk

1 teaspoon vanilla extract

1/2 cup unsweetened cocoa powder

1¼ cups cake flour

1/2 teaspoon salt

1/2 teaspoon baking soda

Preheat oven to 350°. Butter and flour the bottom and sides of a 9-x-13-inch baking dish.

1 In a large bowl, combine butter and sugar. Beat with a mixer until light and fluffy. Add eggs and beat until mixture is light yellow in color. Add milk and vanilla extract and mix until blended.

3 In another bowl, sift together cocoa powder, flour, salt and baking soda.

4 Add flour mixture to egg mixture and mix just until ingredients are blended. Pour batter into prepared pan.

5 Bake for 20 to 25 minutes or until a toothpick inserted into the center comes out clean. Cool in pan on a rack.

Bittersweet Chocolate Layer Cake
Pour batter into two 9-inch round cake pans in step 4. Bake for 18 to 23 minutes.

Bittersweet Chocolate and Walnut Cake
Sprinkle 1/2 cup chopped walnuts on top of cake batter before baking.

Dark Chocolate Cake
Substitute 1¼ cups light brown sugar, packed, for granulated sugar in step 1.

Fresh Apple Walnut Cake

This recipe, at least 3 generations old, came from Italy to America with my grandmother, Angelina. It is sweet and dark and is lovely served warm with vanilla ice cream. Do not rely on the "toothpick test" to test this cake's doneness, as this is a very rich, dense cake.

Servings: 8

1 cup granulated sugar

1 egg, beaten

½ cup butter, melted

1 cup all-purpose flour

1 teaspoon baking soda

½ teaspoon cinnamon

¼ teaspoon salt

2 cups large chunks peeled Granny Smith apples

½ cup chopped walnuts

Preheat oven to 375°. Spray an 8-x-8-inch baking pan with nonstick cooking spray.

1 In a large bowl, combine sugar, egg and butter and mix until smooth.

2 In another bowl, sift together flour, baking soda, cinnamon and salt. Add flour mixture to egg mixture and stir just until mixed.

3 Add apples and walnuts and stir just until mixed. Transfer batter to prepared pan.

4 Bake for 30 minutes. Cool in pan and serve warm or cold; cut into wedges.

Apple Cake
Omit walnuts.

Apple Spice Cake
Omit walnuts. Add ½ teaspoon ground allspice and ¼ teaspoon freshly ground nutmeg in step 2.

Chocolate Walnut Torte

This impressive dessert is rich and satisfying. It is also quick to assemble and virtually foolproof. Changing the types of chocolate and nuts gives you quite a few options for personalizing the recipe. You can also substitute different extracts for vanilla such as almond, peppermint or orange.

Servings: 8-10

½ cup butter

10 oz. bittersweet chocolate

4 eggs

¾ cup sugar

1 teaspoon vanilla extract

¾ cup all-purpose flour

½ teaspoon baking powder

1 cup chopped walnuts

Raspberry Sauce, page 152, optional

Preheat oven to 350°. Spray the bottom and sides of a 9-inch springform pan with nonstick cooking spray.

1 In a medium saucepan, combine butter and chocolate. Heat over medium-low heat, stirring frequently until melted and smooth.

2 In a large bowl, beat eggs until light yellow in color. Add sugar and vanilla and stir until mixed. Add chocolate mixture and stir until well mixed.

3 Add flour, baking powder and walnuts and stir until well mixed. Transfer batter to prepared pan.

4 Bake for 30 to 35 minutes, or until a toothpick inserted into the center comes out clean. Cool cake in pan. Cut into wedges and serve with **Raspberry Sauce**, if desired.

Chocolate Almond Torte
Substitute sliced or slivered almonds for walnuts in step 3.

Chocolate Hazelnut Torte
Substitute chopped hazelnuts for walnuts in step 3.

Butter Cake

Here is a basic recipe for quick butter cake, which you can tailor to your personal taste. It goes together quickly, using ingredients you probably already have in your refrigerator and pantry. Mix it before dinner and you can have dessert waiting for you fresh from the oven.

Servings: 8

1½ cups all-purpose flour

2 teaspoons baking powder

½ teaspoon salt

½ cup sugar

½ cup butter

½ cup milk

1 egg, beaten

Preheat oven to 400°. Spray an 8-x-8-inch baking dish with nonstick cooking spray.

1 In a medium bowl, mix together flour, baking powder, salt and sugar.

2 In a small saucepan, melt butter over low heat. Remove from heat and cool for 5 minutes. Add milk and beaten egg and stir to mix well.

3 Pour butter mixture into bowl with flour mixture and stir until well mixed. Transfer batter to prepared pan

4 Bake for 20 to 25 minutes, or until a toothpick inserted into the center of cake comes out clean. Cool in pan for 5 minutes. Transfer to a rack to cool completely.

Chocolate Chip Butter Cake
Stir 1 cup chocolate chips into batter in step 3. Use semisweet, milk or white chocolate chips or a combination.

Chocolate Chip-Nut Butter Cake
Stir in ¾ cup chocolate chips and ½ cup chopped nuts in step 3. Use semisweet, milk or white chocolate chips. Use walnuts, pecans or almonds.

Desserts

Banana Bread Pudding

In this recipe, bananas are added to a basic bread pudding for a very moist and flavorful version of a family favorite.

Servings: 8

3 ripe bananas, mashed

4 cups white bread pieces

4 eggs

3 cups milk

⅓ cup sugar

½ teaspoon salt

2 teaspoons vanilla extract

Preheat oven to 350°. Spray the bottom and sides of a 9-x-13-inch baking dish with nonstick cooking spray.

1 In a large bowl, combine mashed bananas and bread pieces. Stir well.

2 In another bowl, combine eggs, milk, sugar, salt and vanilla and stir until well blended.

3 Pour milk mixture over bread and bananas and stir to mix well. Transfer bread mixture to prepared pan.

4 Bake until firm and just beginning to brown on top, about 35 to 45 minutes. Cool for 10 minutes before serving. Cool completely and serve chilled.

Banana Honey Bread Pudding
Substitute honey for sugar in step 2.

Spiced Banana Bread Pudding
Add ¼ teaspoon cinnamon and ¼ teaspoon ground nutmeg in step 2.

Chocolate Chip Banana Bread Pudding
Add ½ cup chocolate chips in step 3.

Banana-Raisin Bread Pudding
Substitute cinnamon-raisin bread for white bread in step 1.

Desserts

158

Glazed Pears with Cardamom Cream

This makes an excellent autumn dessert when fresh pears are easily available. It's very easy to prepare and makes a beautiful presentation.

Servings: 4

1 cup
heavy cream

3 tablespoons
confectioners' sugar

½ teaspoon
ground cardamom

4 fresh pears

2 tablespoons
butter

2 tablespoons
brown sugar, packed

1 In a nonmetallic bowl, combine cream and sugar. With a mixer on high speed, beat mixture until stiff peaks form. Add cardamom and mix well. Cover and refrigerate while preparing pears.

2 Core pears and slice lengthwise into wedges. Pat dry with paper towels.

3 In a medium skillet, melt butter over medium-high heat. Add pears and cook, stirring occasionally for about 7 minutes, until juices are released. Sprinkle brown sugar over pears and continue to cook until juices are absorbed and pears are glazed. Take care not to let pears scorch.

4 Place pears on serving plates. Top with cardamom cream and serve immediately.

Glazed Pears with Cinnamon Cream
Substitute freshly ground cinnamon for cardamom in step 1.

Glazed Pears with Ginger Cream
Substitute ground ginger for cardamom in step 1.

Glazed Pears with Nutmeg Cream
Substitute freshly ground nutmeg for cardamom in step 1.

Desserts

Lemon Mousse

You can serve this mousse by itself or top it with a bit of a berry sauce for color and taste contrast. It is perfect for parties, because you can make it early in the day and keep it refrigerated until you are ready to serve.

Servings: 6~8

1/2 cup cold water

2 envelopes
unflavored gelatin

6 egg yolks

1 1/2 cups sugar

1/2 teaspoon salt

1 cup fresh lemon juice

2 tablespoons grated
fresh lemon zest

7 egg whites

2 cups
heavy cream

Raspberry Sauce,
page 151, optional

Please consider using "egg substitutes" when preparing this recipe. Raw eggs have been known to cause salmonella-induced illness in some cases.

1 Place water in a small bowl and sprinkle with gelatin. Let stand for a few minutes to soften.

2 In another bowl, lightly beat egg yolks. Stir in 3/4 cup of the sugar and salt. Add gelatin mixture and stir until mixed. Transfer egg yolk mixture to the top of a double boiler. Cook mixture over simmering water, stirring constantly with a metal spoon, until mixture thickens and coats the back of spoon.

3 Cool mixture for 10 minutes. Add lemon juice and grated zest and stir until well blended. Refrigerate for 10 minutes or until custard just starts to set.

4 In a bowl, whip egg whites until soft peaks form. Add remaining 3/4 cup sugar and whip until mixture forms stiff, glossy peaks. Fold egg white mixture into lemon custard mixture.

5 In another bowl, whip cream until soft peaks form. Fold whipped cream into lemon custard mixture.

6 Transfer mousse to individual ramekins or a large serving bowl. Refrigerate mousse for at least 3 hours. Serve with *Raspberry Sauce*.

Orange Mousse

Substitute freshly squeezed orange juice for lemon juice and grated fresh orange zest for lemon zest in step 3.

Blood Orange Mousse

Substitute freshly squeezed blood orange juice for lemon juice and grated fresh blood orange zest for lemon zest in step 3.

Lime Mousse

Substitute freshly squeezed lime juice for lemon juice and grated fresh lime zest for lemon zest in step 3.

Citrus Mousse

Reduce lemon juice to 1/4 cup. Add 1/4 cup freshly squeezed orange juice, 1/4 cup freshly squeezed lime juice and 1/4 cup freshly squeezed grapefruit juice in step 3. Substitute grated fresh orange zest for lemon zest in step 3.

Pear Clafouti

Clafouti is a dessert that originates from southern France. This version combines fresh fruit and a custard mixture, which is poured on top. Sprinkle the clafouti with confectioners' sugar before serving, if desired.

Servings: 4

2 cups sliced peeled pears

½ teaspoon freshly ground nutmeg

¼ cup plus 3 tablespoons granulated sugar

½ cup milk

½ cup light cream

3 eggs

½ cup all-purpose flour

1 teaspoon vanilla extract

Preheat oven to 350°. Spray the bottom and sides of an 8- or 9-inch pie pan with nonstick cooking spray.

1 In a small bowl, toss together pears, nutmeg and 3 tablespoons sugar. Transfer mixture to pie pan.

2 In a blender container, combine ¼ cup sugar, milk, cream, eggs, flour and vanilla extract. Pulse on high until smooth. Pour custard mixture over pear mixture in pan.

3 Bake until top is light golden brown and puffy, about 35 to 40 minutes. Cool for 5 minutes before serving.

Pear-Blueberry Clafouti
Add 1 cup fresh or thawed frozen blueberries in step 1. Omit nutmeg.

Pear-Raspberry Clafouti
Add 1 cup fresh or thawed frozen raspberries in step 1. Omit nutmeg.

Peach Clafouti
Substitute peeled fresh peaches for pears and freshly ground cinnamon for nutmeg in step 1.

Classic Crème Brulée

Crème Brulée is a rich, comforting dessert. Adding blackberries provides a tart contrast to the sweet and creamy custard.

Servings: 8

3 cups
heavy cream

5 egg yolks

1 egg

⅓ cup
granulated sugar

1 teaspoon
vanilla extract

⅓ cup brown
sugar, packed

1 In a large saucepan, combine cream, egg yolks, egg and sugar. Beat until well mixed.

2 Cook mixture over medium heat, stirring constantly for about 20 minutes. Mixture should be very thick, but take care that it does not boil.

3 Remove mixture from heat. Add vanilla extract and stir until well mixed.

4 Pour custard mixture into 8 shallow ramekins, dividing mixture evenly. Cover ramekins with plastic wrap and refrigerate for at least 6 hours, until well chilled.

6 Preheat broiler. Sift brown sugar over the surface of chilled custard to form an even layer. Broil 4 to 6 inches from heat source for 3 to 5 minutes, until sugar melts and bubbles slightly. Serve immediately or refrigerate until ready to serve.

Blackberry Crème Brulée
Place 1 cup fresh blackberries in ramekins, dividing evenly before adding custard in step 4.

Coffee Crème Brulée
Add 2 tablespoons instant coffee in step 3, stirring until coffee is dissolved.

Desserts

163

Vanilla Intensity Gelato

This extra-rich ice cream has a very, VERY strong vanilla flavor — the name says it all. It makes regular vanilla ice cream seem plain in comparison.

Servings: 8

1½ cups milk

2 vanilla beans, split lengthwise

½ cup sugar

3 egg yolks

1½ cups heavy cream

1 tablespoon vanilla extract

1. In a saucepan, combine milk, vanilla beans and sugar. Cook over medium heat for 15 minutes, stirring frequently until mixture coats the back of a spoon. Take care that mixture does not boil.

2. Remove mixture from heat. Remove vanilla beans and scrape seeds from inside of beans. Return seeds to milk mixture; discard beans.

3. In a small bowl, beat egg yolks until blended. Slowly pour 2 tablespoons of the hot milk mixture into egg yolks, stirring constantly. Pour egg-milk mixture into saucepan with remaining milk mixture, stirring constantly.

4. Cook mixture over medium heat, stirring constantly for 10 minutes or until mixture is thickened and coats the back of a spoon. Transfer mixture to a bowl. Cover and refrigerate for at least 4 hours until cold.

5. Stir cream and vanilla into gelato base and transfer to an ice cream maker. Freeze according to manufacturer's directions. Serve gelato immediately or transfer to a covered container and freeze until ready to serve.

Honey-Vanilla Gelato
Substitute honey for sugar in step 1.

Vanilla-Chocolate Chunk Gelato
Add ½ cup chopped milk chocolate in step 5.

Vanilla-Almond Gelato
Add ½ cup toasted almonds in step 5.

Desserts

164

Cappuccino Gelato

Richer and stronger in flavor than regular coffee ice cream, this recipe is for serious coffee lovers. Although it may seem strange to mix espresso grounds and milk together, it is the best way to obtain a strong coffee flavor.

Servings: 8

2 cups milk

3⁄4 cup ground regular or decaffeinated espresso beans

3 egg yolks

1⁄2 cup sugar

1 cup heavy cream

1 In a saucepan, combine milk and ground coffee. Cook over high heat, stirring frequently, and bring just to a boil.

2 Line a strainer or colander with a paper coffee filter suspended over a large bowl. Pour milk mixture into filter and strain; discard filter and grounds.

3 While milk is filtering, combine egg yolks and sugar in a medium bowl. With a mixer, mix on high speed until egg yolks are light yellow in color.

4 Reduce mixer speed to medium and slowly pour hot milk mixture into egg yolks, mixing constantly until well mixed. Cover and refrigerate for at least 4 hours, until cold.

6 Stir cream into gelato base and transfer to an ice cream maker. Freeze according to manufacturer's directions. Serve gelato immediately or transfer to a covered container and freeze until ready to serve.

Café au Lait Gelato
Substitute French roast coffee beans for espresso beans in step 1.

Flavored Coffee Gelato
Substitute cinnamon or another flavor coffee beans for espresso beans in step 1.

Desserts

Coconut Ice Cream

Coconut ice cream is delicious in the summertime and decadent in the wintertime. Top heaping bowls of ice cream with crushed pineapple for a piña colada sundae.

Servings: 8

1 can (14 oz.) unsweetened coconut milk

1 cup milk

3/4 cup sugar

2 eggs

2 teaspoons vanilla extract

1 cup heavy cream

1/2 cup flaked coconut

1 In a medium saucepan, combine coconut milk, milk, sugar and eggs. Cook over medium heat, stirring constantly until mixture is thickened and coats the back of a spoon. Take care that mixture does not boil.

2 Transfer mixture to a medium bowl. Add vanilla and stir until mixed. Cover and refrigerate for at least 4 hours, preferably overnight until cold and thickened.

3 Stir cream and coconut into ice cream base until well mixed. Transfer to an ice cream maker and freeze according to manufacturer's directions. Serve immediately or transfer to a covered container and freeze until ready to serve.

Toasted Coconut Ice Cream
Substitute toasted coconut for coconut in step 3. Place coconut on a baking sheet and bake in a 350° oven for 20 to 30 minutes, stirring occasionally. Cool completely before adding to ice cream base.

Coconut-Macadamia Ice Cream
Add 1/2 cup chopped macadamia nuts in step 3.

Fresh Raspberry Sorbet

Serve a scoop of this sorbet next to a scoop of *Vanilla Intensity Gelato*, page 149, or other rich vanilla ice cream. You will love the flavor and color contrast.   Servings: 8

1 cup sugar

¾ cup water

¼ teaspoon grated fresh orange zest

4 cups fresh raspberries

1 In a small saucepan, combine sugar and water and bring to a boil over high heat. Mixture will become clear and syrupy.

2 Place orange zest and raspberries in a large heatproof bowl. Pour hot sugar syrup over berries and stir to mix. Cover bowl and refrigerate until cold.

3 Transfer chilled raspberry mixture to a blender container and pulse until mixture is smooth.

4 Strain raspberry mixture through a sieve, pressing to extract as much pulp and juice as possible. Discard seeds left in sieve.

5 Transfer raspberry mixture to an ice cream maker. Freeze according to manufacturer's directions. Serve sorbet immediately or transfer to a covered container and freeze until ready to serve.

Fresh Blackberry Sorbet
Substitute blackberries for raspberries in step 2.

Fresh Strawberry Sorbet
Substitute sliced strawberries for raspberries in step 2.

Fresh Strawberry and Grand Marnier Sorbet
Substitute sliced strawberries for raspberries in step 2. Add 2 tablespoons Grand Marnier just before removing sorbet from ice cream maker in step 5.

Raspberry Sauce

Berry sauces are simple to make and can top everything from bowls of ice cream to slices of cake and wedges of pie.

Makes 2 Cups

2 cups fresh or frozen raspberries

1/2 cup sugar

1 In a medium saucepan, combine frozen berries and sugar. Cook over medium-high heat until berries burst and sugar has dissolved.

2 If you desire a smooth sauce, puree fruit mixture with a blender. Transfer sauce to a bowl, cover and refrigerate until well chilled.

Blackberry Sauce
Substitute fresh or frozen blackberries for raspberries in step 1.

Strawberry Sauce
Substitute sliced fresh or frozen strawberries for raspberries in step 1.

INDEX

A

Almond biscotti 140
Almond chicken salad 58
Appetizers 27-45
  basil mozzarella cheese bites 31
  basil rosemary chicken skewers 39
  cheese and prosciutto polenta
    squares 35
  cheese-stuffed portobello
    mushrooms 36
  classic crab cakes 44
  classic salmon cakes 45
  classic shrimp cakes 45
  green olivada spread 33
  grilled chicken quesadillas 37
  grilled crab quesadillas 37
  grilled quesadillas with salsa cruda
    37
  lemon-basil shrimp 40
  lemon-herb crab legs 40
  lemon-herb scallops 40
  lemon-herb shrimp 40
  lemon rosemary chicken skewers
    39
  mozzarella cheese bites 31
  olivada spread 33
  Parmesan palmiers 32
  pesto palmiers 32
  poached salmon with dill-
    scallion vinaigrette 43
  poached salmon with shallot-
    chive vinaigrette 43
  poached salmon with sweet red
    pepper vinaigrette 42
  pork pillows 34
  pork spring pillows 34
  Provence herbed cheese bites 31
  rosemary chicken skewers 38
  rosemary olivada spread 33
  rosemary pork skewers 39
  sausage polenta squares 35
  sausage-stuffed portobello
    mushrooms 36
  shrimp with lemon aioli 41
  shrimp with lemon-caper aioli 41
  shrimp with lemon-peppercorn aioli
    41
  shrimp pillows 34
  spinach-stuffed portobello
    mushrooms 36
  sun-dried tomato pesto palmiers 32
  sweet red pepper polenta squares 35
  tarragon chicken skewers 39
Apple
  -blackberry pie, spiced 147
  butternut squash soup 68
  cake 155
  cranberry scones 10
  currant scones 10
  currant scones with walnuts 10
  spice cake 155
  walnut cake, fresh 155
Apricot scones 10
Arizona black bean soup 74
Artichoke
  frittata 24
  and pepper Jack rice 89
  rice 89
  risotto 95
  soup, cream of 70
  and tomato salad 51
Asian
  noodle salad 54
  noodle salad with chicken 54
  vegetable soup 66
  vegetable soup with shrimp 66
  vegetable soup with tofu 66
Asparagus risotto 95
Asparagus soup, cream of 70
Autumn honey and pumpkin soup 67
Autumn soup 67

B

Baby bok choy with sesame butter 82
Bacon and jalapeño cornbread 18
Banana
  bread pudding 158
  bread pudding, spiced 158
  honey bread pudding 158
  -raisin bread pudding 158
Basil
  and fresh tomato soup 64
  mozzarella cheese bites 31
  olive oil dipping sauce 30
  roasted tomatoes 83
  rosemary chicken skewers 39

Beef
  filet mignon with garlic herb butter
    133
  garlic, Provençal 129
  garlic, Provençal with leeks 128
  garlic, Provençal with onions 129
  grilled filet mignon with blue cheese
    butter 133
  grilled filet mignon with chile butter 132
  Italian meatball and tortellini soup 75
  Italian meatball soup 75
  Mexican flank steak 130
  Mexican flank steak with peppers 130
  Mexican flank steak with smoky
    onions 130
  pan-seared filet mignon with Brie sauce
    131
  pan-seared filet mignon with
    Gorgonzola sauce 131
  pan-seared filet mignon with herbed
    Brie sauce 131
  pan-seared filet mignon with peppercorn
    Brie sauce 131
  Provençal 129
  roast with autumn vegetables 127
  roast with spring vegetables 127
  roast with winter vegetables 126
  stew, herbed, Italian 125
  stew, Italian 125
  stew with vegetables, Italian 125
  stir-fried with two onions 116
Berry, mixed, cobbler 146
Berry, mixed, shortcakes 153
Biscotti
  almond 140
  crumbles 141
  nutty 140
  pine nut 140
  walnut 140
Biscuits
  buttermilk with chives 11
  classic buttermilk 11
  poppy seed buttermilk 11
  sunflower buttermilk 11
Bittersweet chocolate sin 151
Black bean soup with ham 74
Black bean soup with sausage 74
Blackberry
  -apple pie, spiced 147

Blackberry, continued
   bars 145
   crème brulée 163
   fresh, sorbet 167
   pie 147
   pie, spiced 147
   sauce 168
Blood orange mousse 161
Bread pudding
   banana 158
   banana honey 158
   banana-raisin 158
   chocolate chip banana 158
   spiced banana 158
Breads, quick
   apple cranberry scones 10
   apple currant scones 10
   apple currant scones with walnuts 10
   apricot scones 10
   bacon and jalapeño cornbread 18
   buttermilk biscuits with chives 11
   California strawberry shortcakes 152
   carrot nut spice bread 16
   carrot raisin spice bread 16
   cheddar cheese muffins 14
   cheddar cheese and shallot muffins 15
   cheddar herb bread 17
   classic buttermilk biscuits 11
   green chile cornbread 18
   herb cheese bread 17
   jalapeño cornbread 18
   lemon and berry shortcakes 153
   mixed berry shortcakes 153
   poppy seed buttermilk biscuits 11
   spicy chile cornbread 18
   sun-dried tomato and cheese bread 17
   sunflower buttermilk biscuits 11
   white cheddar cheese muffins 15
   zucchini raisin spice bread 16
Breads, yeast
   cinnamon-pecan rolls 12
   cinnamon-pecan rolls, frosted 13
   cinnamon raisin pecan rolls 13
   egg 19
   honey cinnamon pecan rolls 13
   honey egg 19
   oatmeal honey 20
   oatmeal maple 20
   pecan rolls 13

   pine nut and Parmesan focaccia 21
   raisin egg 19
   rosemary and garlic focaccia 21
   rustic 22
   rustic, with olives 22
   rustic, with walnuts 22
   sun-dried tomato and garlic focaccia 21
Broccoli
   quiche 25
   with sesame butter 82
   soup, cream of 70
Brown and wild artichoke rice 89
Butter cake 157
Butterfinger chip cookies 142
Buttermilk biscuits
   classic 11
   with chives 11
   with poppy seeds 11
   with sunflower seeds 11
Butternut squash soup 68
   with apple 68
   curried 68
   low-fat 68

C

Caesar tortellini salad 56
Caf au lait gelato 165
Cake
   apple 155
   apple spice 155
   bittersweet chocolate 154
   bittersweet chocolate layer 154
   bittersweet chocolate and walnut 154
   butter 157
   chocolate chip butter 157
   chocolate chip-nut butter 157
   dark chocolate 154
   fresh apple walnut 155
Cappuccino gelato 165
Cappuccino mud pie 149
Caribbean
   chicken 114
   pork chops 114
   spareribs 114
Carrot
   nut spice bread 16
   raisin spice bread 16
   soup, cream of 70
Cashew
   chicken salad 58

   chicken salad, creamy 58
   turkey salad 58
Cheddar
   and bacon quiche 25
   cheese muffins 14
   cheese and shallot muffins 15
   herb bread 17
   risotto, baked 94
   white, muffins 15
Cheese
   artichoke and pepper Jack rice 89
   baked cheddar risotto 94
   baked Parmesan risotto 94
   baked Parmesan risotto with chives 94
   baked Romano risotto 94
   bites, basil mozzarella 31
   bites, mozzarella 31
   bites, Provence herbed 31
   cheddar herb bread 17
   cheddar muffins 14
   Florentine Parmesan rice 90
   grilled chicken quesadillas 37
   grilled crab quesadillas 37
   grilled quesadillas with salsa cruda 37
   herb bread 17
   Parmesan brown rice cakes 93
   Parmesan palmiers 32
   Parmesan rice cakes 93
   Parmesan wild rice cakes 93
   and prosciutto polenta squares 35
   rigatoni with sausage, baked 105
   rigatoni with tomatoes, baked 105
   and spinach salad 57
   -stuffed portobello mushrooms 36
   and sun-dried tomato bread 17
   three, rigatoni pasta, baked 105
Chicken
   almond salad 58
   Asian noodle salad with, 54
   braised, with artichokes and tomatoes 118
   braised, with white wine and artichokes 118
   breasts, braised, with artichokes and tomatoes 118
   breasts, grilled, with Caribbean salsa 117
   breasts, grilled, with outback salsa 117
   breasts, grilled, with volcano salsa 117
   Caribbean 114
   cashew salad 58
   cashew salad, creamy 58

Chicken, continued
  fried rice 91
  and mushrooms with brandy sauce 115
  and mushrooms with mustard-brandy
    sauce 115
  with mustard-brandy sauce 115
  with mustard-sherry sauce 115
  pasta puttanesca 104
  and potato salad 59
  quesadillas, grilled 37
  ratatouille 84
  roasted, with chervil 119
  roasted, with fresh sage 119
  roasted, with fresh sage and lemon 119
  roasted, with fresh thyme 119
  roasted, with rice-cashew stuffing
    121
  roasted, with rice-hazelnut stuffing
    121
  roasted, with rice-walnut stuffing 120
  salad, curried 59
  and seafood jambalaya 110
  skewers, basil rosemary 39
  skewers, lemon rosemary 39
  skewers, rosemary 38
  skewers, tarragon 39
  stir-fried with two onions 116
  stir-fried with wine and two onions
    116
  stir-fried with yellow onions 116
Chipotle
  pork ribs, saucy 122
  pork stew 122
  pork and vegetable stew 122
Chocolate
  almond torte 156
  bittersweet, cake 154
  bittersweet, layer cake 154
  bittersweet, sin 151
  bittersweet, and walnut cake 154
  chip banana bread pudding 158
  chip butter cake 157
  chip cookies 142
  chip-nut butter cake 157
  chip-walnut cookies 142
  chunk-vanilla gelato 164
  dark, cake 154
  hazelnut torte 156
  milk, sin 151
  mud pie 149
  walnut torte 156
  white-macadamia cookies 142

  white, sin 150
Chorizo rice 92
Chorizo rice, wildly hot and spicy 92
Cinnamon
  honey pecan rolls 13
  -oatmeal raisin cookies 143
  -pecan rolls 12
  -pecan rolls, frosted 13
  raisin pecan rolls 13
  walnut rolls 13
Citrus confetti cookies 144
Citrus mousse 161
Clam pasta puttanesca 104
Cobbler
  mixed berry 146
  orange-scented berry 146
  peach-berry 146
Coconut
  ice cream 166
  -macadamia ice cream 166
  toasted, ice cream 166
Coffee crème brulée 163
Coffee gelato, flavored 165
Cookies
  almond biscotti 140
  blackberry bars 145
  Butterfinger chip 142
  chocolate chip 142
  chocolate chip-walnut 142
  cinnamon-oatmeal raisin 143
  citrus confetti 144
  fruity oatmeal 143
  lemon 144
  lemon coconut 144
  nutty biscotti 140
  oatmeal 143
  oatmeal raisin 143
  oatmeal-raisin walnut 143
  pine nut biscotti 140
  raspberry bars 145
  strawberry bars 145
  vanilla cream cheese 144
  walnut biscotti 140
  white chocolate-macadamia 142
Corn
  roasted, chowder 72
  roasted, and red pepper chowder 73
  roasted, and spring vegetable
    chowder 73
  smoky roasted, chowder 73
Cornbread
  bacon and jalapeño 18

  green chile 18
  jalapeño 18
  spicy chile 18
Crab
  bisque 77
  cakes, classic 44
  gazpacho 65
  legs, lemon-herb 40
  quesadillas, grilled 37
Crème brulée
  blackberry 163
  classic 163
  coffee 163
Creole
  snapper 111
  sole 111
  turbot 111

D

Desserts 135-168
  apple cake 155
  apple spice cake 155
  banana bread pudding 158
  banana honey bread pudding 158
  banana-raisin bread pudding 158
  bittersweet chocolate cake 154
  bittersweet chocolate layer cake 154
  bittersweet chocolate sin 151
  bittersweet chocolate and walnut cake
    154
  blackberry crème brulée 163
  blackberry pie 147
  blood orange mousse 161
  butter cake 157
  caf au lait gelato 165
  California strawberry shortcakes 152
  cappuccino gelato 165
  cappuccino mud pie 149
  chocolate almond torte 156
  chocolate chip banana bread pudding
    158
  chocolate chip butter cake 157
  chocolate chip-nut butter cake 157
  chocolate hazelnut torte 156
  chocolate mud pie 149
  chocolate walnut torte 156
  citrus mousse 161
  classic crème brulée 163
  coconut ice cream 166
  coconut-macadamia ice cream 166
  coffee crème brulée 163
  dark chocolate cake 154

Desserts, continued
  flavored coffee gelato 165
  fresh apple walnut cake 155
  fresh blackberry sorbet 167
  fresh raspberry sorbet 167
  fresh strawberry and Grand Marnier
    sorbet 167
  fresh strawberry sorbet 167
  glazed pears with cardamom cream
    159
  glazed pears with cinnamon cream
    159
  glazed pears with ginger cream 159
  glazed pears with nutmeg cream
    159
  honey-vanilla gelato 164
  lemon and berry shortcakes 153
  lemon mousse 160
  lime mousse 161
  milk chocolate sin 151
  mixed berry cobbler 146
  mixed berry shortcakes 153
  mocha mud pie 149
  orange mousse 161
  orange-scented berry cobbler 146
  peach-berry cobbler 146
  peach clafouti 162
  pear-blueberry clafouti 162
  pear clafouti 162
  pear-raspberry clafouti 162
  peppermint snow pie 148
  spiced apple-blackberry pie 147
  spiced banana bread pudding 158
  spiced blackberry pie 147
  toasted coconut ice cream 166
  vanilla-almond gelato 164
  vanilla almond snow pie 148
  vanilla-chocolate chunk gelato 164
  vanilla intensity gelato 164
  vanilla snow pie 148
  white chocolate sin 150
Dijon roasted potatoes 87

E

Egg bread 19
Eggplant, in ratatouille 84
Eggplant and vegetable, grilled,
  salad 52
Eggs
  artichoke frittata 24
  broccoli quiche 25
  cheddar and bacon quiche 25

Mexican quiche 25
potato and sausage frittata 23
potato, sausage and onion frittata
  23
potato and zucchini frittata 23
sour cream quiche 25
spinach quiche 25
summer frittata 24
summer frittata with ricotta 24

F

Fettuccine
  with garlic cream sauce 109
  with scallops and garlic cream sauce
    108
  with shrimp and garlic cream sauce
    109
  with tomato-mushroom cream sauce
    107
  with tomato-mushroom and red wine
    sauce 107
  with tomato-mushroom sauce 106
Fiery olive oil dipping sauce 30
Filet mignon
  with garlic herb butter 133
  grilled, with blue cheese butter 133
  grilled, with chile butter 132
  pan-seared, with Brie sauce 131
  pan-seared, with Gorgonzola sauce
    131
  pan-seared, with herbed Brie sauce
    131
  pan-seared, with peppercorn Brie
    sauce 131
Fish: see Seafood
Florentine Parmesan rice 90
Florentine rice 90
Focaccia
  pine nut and Parmesan 21
  rosemary and garlic 21
  sun-dried tomato and garlic 21
Frittata
  artichoke 24
  potato and sausage 23
  potato, sausage and onion 23
  potato and zucchini 23
  summer 24
  summer, with ricotta 24

G

Garlic beef Provençal 129
  with leeks 128

  with onions 129
Garlic olive oil dipping sauce 30
Garlic polenta 88
Gazpacho 65
  blended 65
  crab 65
  shrimp 65
Gelato
  caf au lait 165
  cappuccino 165
  flavored coffee 165
  honey-vanilla 164
  vanilla-almond 164
  vanilla-chocolate chunk 164
  vanilla intensity 164
Greek artichoke and tomato salad 51
Greek-style couscous salad 55
Greek-style couscous salad with sun-
  dried tomatoes 55
Green chile cornbread 18
Green olivada spread 33

H

Ham, in black bean soup 74
Herb(ed)
  -cheese bread 17
  fresh, and cream pasta 97
  fresh, and Parmesan pasta 97
  fresh, pasta 96
  mixed, olive oil dipping sauce 30
  polenta 88
Honey
  cinnamon pecan rolls 13
  egg bread 19
  -mustard pork tenderloin 123
  -vanilla gelato 164

I

Ice cream
  coconut 166
  coconut-macadamia 166
  toasted coconut 166
Ingredients
  omitting and adding 4
  substitution table 3
  substitution tips 2
Italian
  beef stew 125
  beef stew, herbed 125
  beef stew with vegetables 125
  meatball soup 75
  meatball and tortellini soup 75

Italian, continued
    spinach salad 57
    -style couscous salad 55
    tortellini soup 75

J

Jalapeño cornbread 18

L

Leek and fresh tomato soup 64
Lemon
    -basil shrimp 40
    and berry shortcakes 153
    coconut cookies 144
    cookies 144
    -herb crab legs 40
    -herb scallops 40
    -herb shrimp 40
    mousse 160
    rosemary chicken skewers 39
Lime mousse 161
Lobster bisque 77

M

Maple-mustard pork tenderloin 123
Mediterranean cobb salad 53
Mexican flank steak 130
    with peppers 130
    with smoky onions 130
Mexican quiche 25
Milk chocolate sin 151
Mocha mud pie 149
Mozzarella cheese bites 31
Muffins
    cheddar cheese 14
    cheddar cheese and shallot 15
    white cheddar cheese 15
Mushroom soup
    golden 69
    golden with potato 69
    mixed 69
Mushrooms, portobello
    cheese-stuffed 36
    sausage-stuffed 36
    spinach-stuffed 36
Mustard roasted potatoes 87

N

Nutty biscotti 140
Nutty biscotti crumbles 141

O

Oatmeal
    cookies 143
    cookies, fruity 143
    crumbles 141
    honey bread 20
    maple bread 20
    raisin cookies 143
    -raisin walnut cookies 143
Olivada spread 33
Olive oil dipping sauce 30
Orange
    mousse 161
    -mustard pork tenderloin 123
    -scented berry cobbler 146
Oregano roasted tomatoes 83

P

Pancakes
    delicate carrot and potato 86
    delicate potato 86
    delicate potato and chives 86
    rustic potato 86
Parmesan
    brown rice cakes 93
    palmiers 32
    rice cakes 93
    risotto, baked 94
    risotto with chives, baked 94
    wild rice cakes 93
Pasta
    Asian noodle salad 54
    Asian noodle salad with chicken 54
    baked cheese rigatoni with sausage 105
    baked cheese rigatoni with tomatoes 105
    baked three-cheese rigatoni 105
    Caesar salad 56
    Caesar tortellini salad 56
    chicken puttanesca 104
    clam puttanesca 104
    fettuccine with garlic cream sauce 109
    fettuccine with scallops and garlic cream sauce 108
    fettuccine with shrimp and garlic cream sauce 109
    fettuccine with tomato-mushroom and red wine sauce 107
    fettuccine with tomato-mushroom sauce 106

fettuccine with tomato-mushroom cream sauce 107
fresh herb 96
fresh herb and cream 97
fresh herb and Parmesan 97
Greek-style couscous salad 55
Greek-style couscous salad with sun-dried tomatoes 55
Italian meatball and tortellini soup 75
Italian tortellini soup 75
Italian-style couscous salad 55
puttanesca 104
romaine and tortellini salad 56
shrimp puttanesca 104
Thai-peanut noodle salad 54
tomato-mushroom lasagna 107
Peach-berry cobbler 146
Peach clafouti 162
Pear
    -blueberry clafouti 162
    clafouti 162
    -raspberry clafouti 162
Pears
    glazed, with cardamom cream 159
    glazed, with cinnamon cream 159
    glazed, with ginger cream 159
    glazed, with nutmeg cream 159
Pecan rolls 13
Peppermint snow pie 148
Pesto palmiers 32
Pie
    blackberry 147
    cappuccino mud 149
    chocolate mud 149
    mocha mud 149
    peppermint snow 148
    spiced apple-blackberry 147
    spiced blackberry 147
    vanilla almond snow 148
    vanilla snow 148
Pine nut and Parmesan focaccia 21
Pine nut biscotti 140
Polenta 88
    garlic 88
    herbed 88
    squares, cheese and prosciutto 35
    squares, sausage 35
    squares, sweet red pepper 35
    sun-dried tomato 88
Poppy seed buttermilk biscuits 11
Pork
    Caribbean spareribs 114

Pork, continued
   chops and apples with orange-bourbon
     sauce 124
   chops Caribbean 114
   chops with orange sauce 124
   chops with orange-bourbon sauce 124
   fried rice 91
   pillows 34
   ribs, saucy chipotle 122
   and seafood jambalaya 110
   skewers, rosemary 39
   spring pillows 34
   stew, chipotle 122
   tenderloin, honey-mustard 123
   tenderloin, maple-mustard 123
   tenderloin, orange-mustard 123
   and vegetable stew, chipotle 122
Potato(es)
   buttermilk and bacon mashed 85
   buttermilk mashed 85
   Dijon roasted 87
   mustard roasted 87
   pancakes with carrot, delicate 86
   pancakes with cheddar, delicate 86
   pancakes with chives, delicate 86
   pancakes, delicate 86
   pancakes, rustic 86
   rosemary and mustard roasted 87
   and sausage frittata 23
   sausage and onion frittata 23
   sour cream and chive mashed 85
   sour cream mashed 85
   and zucchini frittata 23
Provence herbed cheese bites 31

Q
Quesadillas
   grilled chicken 37
   grilled crab 37
   grilled with salsa cruda 37
Quiche
   broccoli 25
   cheddar and bacon 25
   Mexican 25
   sour cream 25
   spinach 25

R
Raisin egg bread 19
Raspberry
   bars 145
   fresh, sorbet 167

sauce 168
Ratatouille 84
   chicken 84
   shrimp 84
Red chard risotto 95
Red pepper
   and roasted corn chowder 73
   roasted, soup, cream of 71
   soup, cream of, fiery 71
Red wine and olive oil dipping sauce 30
Rice
   artichoke 89
   artichoke risotto 95
   articoke and pepper Jack 89
   asparagus risotto 95
   baked cheddar risotto 94
   baked Parmesan risotto 94
   baked Parmesan risotto with chives
     94
   baked Romano risotto 94
   brown and wild artichoke 89
   brown Parmesan cakes 93
   cakes 93
   cakes, Parmesan 93
   -cashew stuffing 121
   chicken fried 91
   chorizo 92
   Florentine 90
   Florentine Parmesan 90
   -hazelnut stuffing 121
   and Italian-style sausage 92
   pork fried 91
   red chard risotto 95
   sausage 92
   shrimp fried 91
   spinach risotto 95
   Swiss chard 90
   vegetable fried 91
   -walnut stuffing 120
   wild Parmesan cakes 93
   wildly hot and spicy chorizo 92
Rolls
   cinnamon-pecan 12
   cinnamon raisin pecan 13
   cinnamon walnut 13
   frosted cinnamon pecan 13
   honey cinnamon pecan 13
   pecan 13
Romaine and tortellini salad 56
Romano risotto, baked 94
Rosemary
   chicken skewers 38

and garlic focaccia 21
and mustard roasted potatoes 87
olivada spread 33
pork skewers 39
Rustic bread 22
with olives 22
with walnuts 22

S
Salads 47-59
   almond chicken 58
   artichoke and tomato 51
   Asian noodle 54
   Asian noodle with chicken 54
   Caesar tortellini 56
   cashew chicken 58
   cashew turkey 58
   chicken and potato 59
   creamy cashew chicken 58
   curried chicken 59
   curried turkey 59
   Greek artichoke and tomato 51
   Greek-style couscous 55
   Greek-style couscous with sun-dried
     tomatoes 55
   grilled eggplant and vegetable 52
   grilled vegetable 52
   herbed grilled vegetable 52
   Italian spinach 57
   Italian-style couscous 55
   Mediterranean cobb 53
   pasta Caesar 56
   romaine and tortellini 56
   San Francisco cobb 53
   simply perfect 50
   simply perfect summer 50
   simply perfect vegetable 50
   Southwestern cobb 53
   spinach and bacon 57
   spinach and cheese 57
   Thai-peanut noodle 54
   tomato and hearts of palm 51
   turkey and potato 59
Salmon
   cakes, classic 45
   poached with dill-scallion vinaigrette 43
   poached with shallot-chive vinaigrette 43
   poached with sweet red pepper
     vinaigrette 42
San Francisco cobb salad 53

Sauce
    blackberry 168
    dipping, aioli 41
    dipping, basil olive oil 30
    dipping, fiery olive oil 30
    dipping, garlic olive oil 30
    dipping, mixed herb 30
    dipping, olive oil 30
    dipping, red wine and olive oil 30
    raspberry 168
    strawberry 168
Saucy chipotle pork ribs 122
Sausage
    with baked cheese rigatoni 105
    in black bean soup 74
    Italian-style and rice 92
    polenta squares 35
    and potato frittata 23
    rice 92
    and seafood jambalaya 110
    -stuffed portobello mushrooms 36
Scallops
    and fettuccine with garlic cream sauce
        108
    lemon herb 40
Scones
    apple cranberry 10
    apple currant 10
    apple currant with walnuts 10
    apricot 10
Seafood
    bisque 77
    and chicken jambalaya 110
    clam pasta puttanesca 104
    classic crab cakes 44
    classic salmon cakes 45
    classic shrimp cakes 45
    crab bisque 77
    crab gazpacho 65
    Creole snapper 111
    Creole sole 111
    Creole turbot 111
    fettuccine with scallops and garlic
        cream sauce 108
    fettuccine with shrimp and garlic
        cream sauce 109
    grilled crab quesadillas 37
    grilled tuna with caper-lemon butter
        113
    grilled tuna with cilantro-lime butter
        113

grilled tuna with parsley-lemon butter
    113
jambalaya 110
lemon-basil shrimp 40
lemon-herb crab legs 40
lemon-herb scallops 40
lemon-herb shrimp 40
lobster bisque 77
poached salmon with dill-scallion
    vinaigrette 42
poached salmon with shallot-chive
    vinaigrette 42
poached salmon with sweet red
    pepper vinaigrette 42
and pork jambalaya 110
and sausage jambalaya 110
shrimp bisque 76
shrimp gazpacho 65
shrimp pasta puttanesca 104
shrimp pillows 34
shrimp with lemon aioli 41
shrimp with lemon-caper aioli 41
shrimp with lemon-peppercorn aioli
    41
trout with balsamic basil sauce 112
trout with balsamic lemon sauce 112
trout with balsamic sauce 112
Shortbread crumbles 141
Shrimp
    in Asian vegetable soup 66
    bisque 76
    cakes, classic 44
    and fettuccine with garlic cream
        sauce 109
    fried rice 91
    gazpacho 65
    with lemon aioli 41
    lemon-basil 40
    with lemon-caper aioli 41
    lemon-herb 40
    with lemon-peppercorn aioli 41
    pasta puttanesca 104
    pillows 34
    ratatouille 84
Side dishes 79-97
Sorbet
    fresh blackberry 167
    fresh raspberry 167
    fresh strawberry 167
    fresh strawberry and Grand Marnier
        167

Soups 61-77
    apple butternut squash 68
    Arizona black bean 74
    Asian vegetable with shrimp 66
    Asian vegetable 66
    Asian vegetable with tofu 66
    autumn 67
    autumn honey and pumpkin 67
    black bean with ham 74
    black bean with sausage 74
    blended gazpacho 65
    butternut squash 68
    butternut squash soup, low-fat 68
    crab bisque 77
    crab gazpacho 65
    cream of artichoke 70
    cream of asparagus 70
    cream of broccoli 70
    cream of carrot 70
    cream of roasted red pepper 71
    curried butternut squash 68
    fiery cream of red pepper 71
    fiery cream of yellow pepper 71
    fresh corn chowder 73
    fresh heirloom tomato 64
    fresh tomato 64
    fresh tomato and basil 64
    fresh tomato and leek 64
    gazpacho 65
    golden mushroom 69
    golden mushroom and potato 69
    Italian meatball 75
    Italian meatball and tortellini 75
    Italian tortellini 75
    lobster bisque 77
    mixed mushroom 69
    roasted corn chowder 72
    roasted corn and red pepper chowder
        73
    seafood bisque 77
    shrimp bisque 76
    shrimp gazpacho 65
    smoky roasted corn chowder 73
    spring vegetable 67
    spring vegetable and roasted corn
        chowder 73
    winter vegetable 67
Sour cream quiche 25
Southwestern cobb salad 53
Spicy chile cornbread 18
Spinach
    and bacon salad 57

Spinach, continued
  and cheese salad 57
  Florentine Parmesan rice 90
  Florentine rice 90
  Italian salad 57
  quiche 25
  risotto 95
  -stuffed portobello mushrooms 36
Spreads
  green olivada 33
  olivada 33
  rosemary olivada 33
Spring vegetable soup 67
Strawberry
  bars 145
  fresh and Grand Marnier sorbet 167
  fresh, sorbet 167
  sauce 168
  shortcakes, California 152
Stuffing
  rice-cashew 121
  rice-hazelnut 121
  rice-walnut 120
Sugar snap peas with sesame butter
  82
Summer frittata 24
Summer frittata with ricotta 24
Sun-dried tomato
  and cheese bread 17
  and garlic focaccia 21
  pesto palmiers 32
  polenta 88
Sunflower buttermilk biscuits 11
Sweet red pepper polenta squares 35
Swiss chard rice 90

T

Tarragon chicken skewers 39
Tarragon roasted tomatoes 83
Thai-Peanut noodle salad 54
Three-cheese rigatoni pasta, baked
  105
Tomato(es)
  basil roasted 83
  fresh, and basil soup 64
  fresh, and leek soup 64
  fresh, soup 64
  and hearts of palm salad 51
  heirloom, fresh, soup 64
  -mushroom lasagna 107
  oregano roasted 83
  oven-roasted 83

  tarragon roasted 83
Trout
  with balsamic basil sauce 112
  with balsamic lemon sauce 112
  with balsamic sauce 112
Tuna
  grilled, with caper-lemon butter 113
  grilled, with cilantro-lime butter 113
  grilled, with parsley-lemon butter 113
Turkey
  cashew salad 58
  and potato salad 59
  salad, curried 59

V

Vanilla
  -almond gelato 152
  almond snow pie 148
  -chocolate chunk gelato 152
  cream cheese cookies 144
  intensity gelato 152
  snow pie 148
Vegetable(s)
  autumn, with beef roast 127
  and chipotle pork stew 122
  and eggplant, grilled, salad 52
  fried rice 91
  grilled, salad 52
  herbed and grilled, salad 52
  in Italian beef stew 125
  salad, simply perfect 50
  soup, Asian 66
  soup, Asian with shrimp 66
  soup, Asian with tofu 66
  soup, spring 67
  soup, winter 67
  spring, and roasted corn chowder
    73
  spring, with beef roast 127
  winter, with beef roast 126

W

Walnut biscotti 140
White cheddar cheese muffins 15
White chocolate-macadamia cookies
  142
White chocolate sin 150
Winter vegetable soup 67

Y

Yellow pepper soup, cream of, fiery 71

Z

Zucchini raisin spice bread 16
Zucchini with sesame butter 82